FORTITUDE FOREVER

A Memoir and 12 Lessons for Those
Thinking of Giving Up

SUYASH SAURABH SINGH

BLUEROSE PUBLISHERS
India | U.K.

Copyright © Suyash Saurabh Singh 2024

All rights reserved by author. No part of this publication may be reproduced, stored in a retrieval system or transmitted in any form or by any means, electronic, mechanical, photocopying, recording or otherwise, without the prior permission of the author. Although every precaution has been taken to verify the accuracy of the information contained herein, the publisher assumes no responsibility for any errors or omissions. No liability is assumed for damages that may result from the use of information contained within.

BlueRose Publishers takes no responsibility for any damages, losses, or liabilities that may arise from the use or misuse of the information, products, or services provided in this publication.

For permissions requests or inquiries regarding this publication, please contact:

BLUEROSE PUBLISHERS
www.BlueRoseONE.com
info@bluerosepublishers.com
+91 8882 898 898
+4407342408967

ISBN: 978-93-6452-583-1

Cover Design: Sadhna Kumari
Typesetting: Pooja Sharma

First Edition: August 2024

This book is dedicated to you, Papa.

Your presence is cosmic,

I am glad I can never grow out of it.

Acknowledgment

This book is dedicated to my father, Lt. Mr. Dushyant Singh. The fortitude and perseverance he demonstrated in his own battles and selfless service to others will forever be my inspiration.

I am deeply grateful to my sister, Dr. Pranjul Singh, who has always been my rock. Thank you for your endless patience with me, your sense of humor, and your unconditional love. I am indebted to my mother, Mrs. Dipti Singh, for the countless selfless sacrifices she has made for our family. I also want to thank my brother-in-law, Dr. Shubham Maurya, for the endless love, support, and inspiration he has offered me.

I am immensely grateful to Niks for believing in me and encouraging me to complete the first draft in time. And the team at Bluerose for supporting through all the stages of actualizing this dream of mine.

I am grateful to my friends Ashutosh and Siddhartha for the strength they continue to provide in my life. Akanksha and Arpita, for being the constants in this ever-changing life. I guess we are all destined to grow old together.

I am deeply grateful to Mrs. Urmila Sharma for believing in me and supporting me like a second mother. You will always hold a special place in my life. I also want to thank my brother Shashwat and my friend Mrigank, for their kindness and immense support during one of the toughest times in my life.

I am also indebted to my friend Vidushi for her constant support and kindness. You are like an elder sister to me, and I am immensely grateful to you. I am grateful to my friends, Aviral, Jayant, Aditya and Akash for their thoughtful suggestions and constant support in my life. I also want to thank Shubham Kamboj and Shehryar Khan for their valuable guidance and belief in me during college. Your support helped me never give up on my unconventional ideas, and I will forever be grateful for that. I am also grateful to Mr. Manpreet Singh Bajwa for the opportunities, and endless support he provided as a mentor during college. And I want to especially thank Vibhor Bhatnagar for supporting my ideas. Many unbelievable experiences would not have been possible without your belief in what we were doing.

I want to extend a special thanks to three people: Gaurav Arya (YouTube: GauravAryaTv) for the unexpected and unfiltered conversation on a random evening in January 2024. That conversation was inspiring and pivotal, and I am grateful for it. Aman Chak (Instagram: aman.liftheavy) for practically changing my life through your extraordinary expertise. Simran Kaur (Instagram: thebrewingsocials) for providing your valuable guidance and selfless support in my projects. I owe you lots of chai!

And last but not least, I want to thank my readers. It is my sincere hope that this book will provide you with the inspiration and strength you are looking for.

Thank you all.

The Lows
don't feel so still,
spilling my dreams,
from the edge of reality,
on the ground of broken will,
they walk along,
and drag me down,
on the road that goes uphill,
for all the stories,
for all the storms,
and for those who left unfulfilled,
I can tell you,
What I see in the dark,
No, the lows,
They don't feel so still.

-Suyash

Preface

Your heart is bruised and battered. You might be exhausted from pouring all your energy and soul into crafting beautiful memories, only to watch them crumble into painful experiences. Life is meant to have its highs and lows, but why do you always end up sifting through the ashes of your most cherished and foundational dreams? It feels like some unseen force is relentlessly trying to bring you to your knees, urging you to give up and abandon your dreams. It's not just the isolated failures, but the relentless pattern of heartbreak that makes you want to stop trying. No one's advice seems to resonate because it feels like no one has faced as many defeats as you have.

I feel your pain, deeply.

In this book, I have shared my own personal story, which honestly was daunting. It requires a willingness to be vulnerable, to expose wounds that have long been hidden, to relive moments of deep pain and joy, and to open yourself up to the judgment of strangers. Yet, it is through this act of sharing that I can authentically form a connection with you. To tell you that,

I see you;

I understand you.

So, let me win your trust and then present to you the principles with which I have nurtured Fortitude in my life.

In the first section, I open up about my life's journey. It begins with the pressures of academic achievement and the responsibilities I bore at a young age. These formative experiences paved the way for a life filled with both heartache and triumph. From the grief of losing loved ones and battling health challenges to the pain of betrayal and the joy of self-discovery, each chapter offers a raw and honest portrayal of my struggles and growth. My hope is that these stories will resonate with you, showing that we are all connected through our shared experiences of hardship and resilience.

The second section translates these personal experiences into practical lessons. Here, I draw on psychological research and philosophical insights to provide you with tools and strategies to cultivate resilience and inner strength. This part of the book is designed to empower you to transform adversity into growth, to find meaning in suffering, and to live a life of purpose and strength.

But let me be clear about what this book is not. It is not a collection of quick fixes or superficial platitudes. It does not offer easy answers or guarantee a life free of pain. This book is not for those seeking to escape their struggles but for those willing to confront them head-on. Those who have the spirit to fight. It is for those who understand that true fortitude is forged in the fire of adversity, not in its avoidance.

So, if you are ready to join me, to delve into the depths of your soul and uncover the strength that lies within, then let us begin. While you read this book, you can also check the official website www.fortitudeforever.com or my Instagram @fortitudeforeverpodcast for connecting with me personally.

May this book be a source of warmth for you while you fight in your life and a reminder that, no matter the obstacles, we all have the capacity to endure and thrive. Together, we will emerge not unscathed, but stronger, wiser, and more resilient than before to live our lives with **Fortitude Forever.**

With heartfelt gratitude,

Suyash

Contents

Section I 1

Two Marks 2

I Won't Make It..12

Everyone Zigs, You Zag! 17

Smell The Coffee and Wake Up! 22

No Excuses 28

4-Minute 33-Second..34

I Will Be Reponsible!..39

Everything That Matters to You 46

Fortitude Forever 55

Section II 59

1. Should I Give Up?..60

2. The Blueprint Within: Your Values & Vision..............68

3. Chase Your Goals, Don't Get Chased by Anti-Goals! ...80

4. Believe That You Have What It Takes........................87

5. Adapt To Whatever You Are Escaping From...............94

6. Seek Joy, Not Pleasure..105

7. Accept Grief as the Final Stage of Love......................112

8. Build Physical Strength as Well.................................117

9. Produce High-Quality Work 121
10. Mix Your Obsession with Patience 127
11. Love Yourself and Your People from Your Bare Soul 134
12. Cherish the Neutral Moments in Life 144

Section I

Two Marks

It was an important evening in April 2016. I was anxiously comparing the answers I had jotted down during my JEE Mains exam to a solution key posted online by a coaching institute. Initially, as I checked off the answers and found them correct, my heart soared with hope. Finally, I thought to myself, my hard work was paying off. I could feel a tangible sense of progress – an elusive thing in the rat race that is the Indian education system.

But as I continued to tally the later answers, a shadow of doubt crept in. By the end, I nervously calculated my score. At first, it surpassed the estimated cutoff, and with it came what felt like a perfect conclusion: my father's struggle, confined to the house for eight years, my mother's relentless dedication to his care, and my sister's unwavering support, sacrificing a substantial portion of her stipend to help me prepare for this exam, allowing me to focus away from home and its burdens for the past year.

But, that's not how life works. Well, at least not mine.

As I progressed, I discovered that most of the answers I had marked towards the end were incorrect. With each wrong tick, my initial elation turned to dismay, echoing the sinking feeling of a dreadful reality. My score fell just two marks shy of the cutoff line.

I sat there, my legs numb, my feet icy, with sweat beading across my face. Each beat of my heart echoed loudly in the silence. Frozen in place, I couldn't move forward, grappling with the weight of this newly discovered fate pressing down upon me, unsure how to face the rest of my life from that moment on.

Consistent Handwriting

In my childhood, I was a happy kid who always just wanted to play, and I found ways to make more time for it. I used to persuade my classmates and friends to complete my notes for me, not as a bully but because I had a knack for connecting with them. In return, I ensured they had a great time at school. I had many friends, and my main focus was leading them and playing during recess. I came up with the most fun games, and was always the one to make sure everyone was having a great time. I often threw away the food my mom lovingly packed every day for me, just to have more time for mindlessly running through the corridors of the school during our lunch break. Each of my notebooks had different handwriting because I delegated them to various friends. When exams approached, I planned meticulously—while brushing my teeth in the morning, I would recall which notebook belonged to which friend and strategize how to present each subject to my father, who was intent on helping me prepare for the exams. From the second standard until the sixth, I continued my cute little scheme. But at home, things were changing in ways I didn't fully understand.

It all began when I was in the third standard, when my father was hospitalized for the first time. When you're a kid, you tend to believe that your parents are immortal. It's not something you consciously think about, but you feel it. But things changed for me that day. For the first time in my life, both my mom and dad were absent, leaving my maternal aunt to care for my sister and me. My sister is five years older than me, and had a very different approach to education than I did. Instead of being a wild ape running through the corridors, she was a brilliant prodigy who always ranked first in her class. She had a strict rule at home: no disturbances during her study time.

Meanwhile, my father, despite being in the hospital, was still managing his wholesale business over the phone. The business needed someone to handle transactions—handing over products, collecting payments, and keeping records.

At just eight years old, I took on this responsibility.

As I juggled these new responsibilities, I couldn't help but feel the absence of my parents keenly. Despite the arrangement being initially temporary, lasting just a month, it marked the beginning of a newfound resilience in my life.

I still vividly remember waking up one night to see my father being brought back on a stretcher after his first surgery. It was late, and I also happened to have a fever that night. Despite feeling terribly sick, I remember being praised for keeping the notebook intact, with all the transactions noted properly — and with just one consistent handwriting! They were proud of me, and that was the best feeling in the world.

Life had taken a sharp turn, and this new reality defined much of my childhood. I didn't fully grasp what was happening and school became my refuge.

It was the one place I could find solace and happiness, where I could still be a kid. Every time the doorbell rang, I knew I had to race to the door to answer it. I had to constantly check if my father needed anything and swiftly fetch it for him to spare him from painful movements. The business now operated from home, so I was always on hand to deliver products to clients. Over the years, my father underwent multiple surgeries, most of which were just the result of the doctor's incompetency.

I remember when I was in 10th grade, my elder sister was away at college, and my maternal grandmother came to care for me while my father was hospitalized for yet another surgery. It wasn't long before I realized she needed care herself; she would hallucinate while resting, which was quite unsettling and scared me at the time. I took on the responsibility of preparing meals with her for my mom and dad, who were at the hospital. It was the first time I cooked rotis. Twice a day, I would pack the meals and ride my bicycle to the hospital to deliver them.

Home had already become a lonely place since my sister left for higher studies a year earlier. Now, school, once my last refuge and source of joy, had turned dreadful because of bullying from my math teacher. I still remember being slapped in front of the class simply because I didn't perform well on a random test—due to spending the previous day preparing and delivering food to the hospital. He's the reason I still dislike mathematics.

During that difficult phase, the only thing that offered me peace and calm at the end of each day was writing poetry.

Allowed to stay up late to study in high school, I found comfort in the quiet of the night. In those moments of absolute silence, I felt the rhythm of poetry flowing from within me. I would write these verses in cursive handwriting, cherishing them as they reflected my deepest emotions and provided me companionship—a true friend indeed.

When I finished school, my sister had already made plans to take me away from home so I could solely focus on preparing for the country's toughest exam. I had to crack it. She understood that if I stayed home, I would continue to support my parents, especially my father, with every little thing, possibly hindering my own future prospects. It was a difficult decision for my father, who was deeply attached to me emotionally. Despite his heartache, he knew it was necessary and eventually agreed to let me go.

I learned later from my mom that he cried for hours on the day I left home for the first time.

Your Ticket Has Been Cancelled

I ended up in another city, and soon after, my sister joined me as she started her PhD at IIT, in the same city. This year became incredibly important in my life. After four years apart, having my sister in the same city was a huge relief. Every Sunday, I eagerly looked forward to our time together. I had missed her so much during our time apart, and being with her again brought me comfort and stability.

During that time, my sister became my rock, my mentor and caregiver. Despite financial limitations, she ensured I had everything I needed. She used a significant part of her stipend to buy me clothes, give me pocket money, and meet all my needs except for the coaching fees. Her support meant everything to me during that time.

I came here with two clear goals: to transform my life entirely and to reassure my father that my future would be secure.

In the eyes of every Indian parent, success in that particular exam ensures this security. While I didn't fully grasp why he needed that reassurance, like many students, I assumed it was about pride and justifying the hefty fees he had paid over the past two years, with more to come this year. However, the day that would change everything for me was yet to come.

It was a week before Rakshabandhan, a time when everyone was making plans to return home as the coaching institutes had announced a week-long holiday. I excitedly informed my sister, who promptly booked my train tickets. However, just half an hour later, I got a notification from the railways informing me that those tickets had been cancelled.

Confused, I asked my sister about it. She explained that our parents wanted me to focus on my studies for now and postpone my visit, as they were caught up with something and were busy. I was taken aback! I couldn't believe it. This was my first time away from home, and after months of being apart, they suddenly wanted me to cancel my plans to visit them? I couldn't accept it, so I decided to call my maternal grandmother. She was known for her honesty even when firmly told to keep quiet about something. After some coaxing, she revealed to me the truth: my father was undergoing another risky surgery, one that could potentially threaten his life.

He had chosen not to tell me because he didn't want me to worry and lose focus on my studies.

I knew my father well enough to understand how much he must have wanted me by his side during such a critical time. Yet, he had made the difficult decision to keep me away, sacrificing his own comfort and desire for my future.

Four Cups of Tea After Dinner

I cried for hours, the intensity of my emotions now tenfold as I write about it. The realization that my father might not survive, and that he prioritized securing my future over having his family by his side when he was looking at death in the eye profoundly changed me.

That day marked a permanent shift in my understanding, finally illuminating everything I had experienced since childhood.

He emerged safely from the surgery, and it was only afterward that we received word from their end about how it went.

I was now utterly determined to ace this exam. I banished any thoughts of pleasure or comfort from my mind, staying up all night to study and grabbing just a few hours of sleep before morning coaching sessions.

I distanced myself from my friends and avoided making new ones. Initially, there were hurtful comments written on my hostel door because I chose not to socialize with anyone. However, as time went on, some of them were inspired by my dedication and sought genuine connection with me, hoping to boost their own focus and goals.

During winter nights, I would wear just a cotton vest inside my room to stay awake in the cold weather. I also drank four cups of tea after dinner for the same reason—to help keep me alert and focused.

Things were going well, and I distinctly remember feeling proud of myself for not joining the New Year's Party happening right above my ceiling on the terrace. Instead, I welcomed 2016 by staying focused on my goal and studying just as diligently as I did every night.

Around 4:30 AM on January 1st, 2016, after the party had ended and my studies for the night were done, it was finally time for me to sleep.

I stepped out onto the terrace in my vest, leaning against the railing, filled with pride and completely focused on my goal. I remember saying aloud, "Welcome, 2016: the year my life will change forever!"

Despite the cold, I felt happily exhausted. I returned to my room and slept soundly. When I woke up, I felt so dizzy that just reaching my room's door seemed like a daunting task.

Accha, Didi ki bhi Care Karni Hoti Hai!

I was running a high fever and had a persistent cough. The fever persisted for the next two months, during which I was on constant medication. The combination of poor nutrition, lack of sleep, and ongoing medication left my body so weakened that it struggled to recover for those two long months.

At first, I battled my illness alone, but eventually, my sister took me to IIT where I stayed with her for about 15 days. However, when my condition didn't improve, I had to return home. One major reason for leaving the IIT campus was being expelled in the middle of the night for staying there without proper authorization. It was disheartening that the institute I was working so hard to enter had ejected me under those circumstances.

When I was thrown out of the campus, I was accompanied by a very important man in my life who took me back to my hostel on the other side of the city. He made sure I was comfortable and tucked me into bed.

He asked me not to tell my sister everything that had happened at the campus because he knew it would worry her greatly. This man later became my brother-in-law, and it felt perfectly fitting. His actions taught me the importance of caring for my sister's peace of mind and well-being – something that I easily took for granted at times.

I remember the exact words that popped in my head, ***"Achha, Didi ki bhi care karni hoti hai!"*** (Oh, my elder sister needs care too!)

My elder sister has always been my rock, my guardian. I have always looked up to her for everything I have needed in life, but she herself was a human, she needed care too. I slept happy that night, knowing that she has found someone who saw that right away.

Mock and Panic

Back at home, with just a month left before the exam, I gathered myself and my notes, determined to make the most of the time left. Despite feeling scared, I made a conscious decision not to dwell on past challenges. Instead, I focused on utilizing whatever time remained to succeed.

Failure was simply not an option for me.

The day before the exam, I took mock tests and performed well enough to feel confident about being eligible for the actual JEE Advanced exam a month later. But then I remembered my sister's score and used it as a benchmark.

I realized I needed to perform even better in the exam than I was doing in the mock tests, just one day before the actual exam. This mindset was a recipe for failure.

During the exam, I carefully worked through many questions, taking my time to solve them properly. However, I became fixated on my goal to outperform my mock test scores.

The teacher in the classroom was shouting, adding to my stress and making it difficult to stay calm and focused. In a panic, I began marking answers that seemed "close enough" to my calculations. It was no better than "guessing randomly" because this was not an easy exam.

I ended up marking more answers than I should have, all because I was fixated on one goal: to surpass my mock test scores. As a result, I fell short by just 2 marks, missing out on the chance for a significantly different life path for the next four years.

I Won't Make It

The news deeply distressed my father. Up until then, he had been grappling with numerous medical issues and mobility challenges due to extensive medication and multiple surgeries. My failure triggered a disturbing psychological response in him. He began experiencing panic attacks, convinced during each episode that he was going to die. I sat beside him through each attack, monitoring his blood pressure, fetching his medications, and reassuring him that everything would be okay.

During those attacks, something profound that would shape my life forever occurred: my father would confide what seemed like his last words to me in those solitary moments.

With tears in his eyes, his head resting on my lap and his hand in mine, he expressed, "*I won't make it, beta. I am not going to be here. Take care of your mother, always keep her with you, continue with the business, and try to get into a local university for your studies. Get your sister married to the person of her choice.*"

No Witnesses

I was barely 19 years old at the time. It was the first time in my life I had worked so hard for something, only to fail. This failure wasn't just about my career; it was witnessing my father in such a miserable state. Until then, I had the reputation of someone who didn't take their studies seriously. Over the past year, I had poured everything I had into my preparation, but there was no one to witness my hard work. Relatives began to blame me for my father's condition, although their opinions ultimately didn't matter to me. Despite this, I struggled to make sense of the situation.

My sister told me to accept that everyone faces failure, despite how terrible it felt in the moment—it's part of life. She reassured me that it was okay, and whatever was happening wasn't my fault. She encouraged me to focus on figuring out what I wanted to do next and to give my complete attention to that. Her advice about "choosing how you respond" prompted me to reflect deeply on my situation. I made a decision to start from the basics and explore what was going on inside me.

I embarked on a journey to understand who I truly am and what I genuinely desire.

During this quest, I discovered the concepts of "personal values" and "visualization." I took time to complete exercises to identify my personal values in life. I also practiced meditation and visualized the future I envisioned for myself. I made sure to write everything down, detailing the specific scenes I hoped to experience in my life.

Alongside these visions, I listed the virtues that I resolved never to compromise on, regardless of any challenges or temptations. This might seem like a very trivial thing to do and know about yourself. But at the face of the intense adversity I was facing in my life, those words and information about my inner self were everything to me.

Nobody Cares, Bro!

I then started putting my plans into action. The first step was finding a college that could lead to a decent job offer. The second step was aiming to impact people's lives, helping them understand how to handle such complex situations in life. And for that I had to figure out a lot about life, myself. Nevertheless, I began working on launching a blog. After much contemplation, I settled on the name: "Awesome Life Geek." As in, "a person who is obsessed about creating an awesome life".

I had an android tablet at that time, and I setup a simple blogspot website using that. I designed a logo and prepared the about section of the website with great care. During that period, I had drifted away from many of my friends due to my intense focus on exam preparation over the past year. I vividly recall scrolling through my entire contact list, feeling disconnected from every single person, unable to find someone to call and share what was happening in my life.

However, during this time, a school friend reached out to me—not out of genuine concern, but seemingly to mock my setback. Many of my peers had already enrolled in colleges a year earlier, right after school, adding to the sense of isolation I felt. They ridiculed my belief that taking a gap year could lead to success in cracking the exam. Initially, I misunderstood their intentions and believed they were reaching out to assist me in finding a good college. In an attempt to update them on my progress, I shared the link to my blog.

He went through it and replied "Nobody Will Care About This".

I persisted with my work on the blog and proudly showed it to my father. When he asked if I had created the website myself, I saw hope rekindle in his eyes. From then on, I enthusiastically shared every detail about the blog—updating him on new followers on the Facebook page and discussing my plans for its future.

Gradually, he began to trust in my abilities and recognized the sincerity in my efforts.

Kabhi Kisi Ke Kandhe Par Hath Mat Rakhna!

Within a few weeks, I discovered a private college with affordable fees that boasted a strong track record of attracting reputable companies for campus placements. I overheard my father telling my sister over the phone, "I know if he gets the opportunity to sit in a job interview, he has what it takes to succeed, for sure! I trust that he will make something of himself. He will be sorted."

Those words weren't just spoken; I witnessed a noticeable improvement in his health afterward. There were fewer panic attacks and a more positive outlook on life.

I had found the key: Chase the ideal future I visualized, Never compromise on my values, and share every little positive detail about my journey with my father everyday to keep him involved and give him daily dose of hope that I would find stability and success in my life.

As I went to the college alone to secure admission, for the next four years, no one from my family visited the campus. However, as I prepared to leave, my father hugged me and said, *"**Kabhi kisi ke kandhe par hath rkhke mat chalna, aese bano ki log tmhare kandhe par hath rakhein.** Aur jiss bhi sheher me naukri lena, vahi ghar lenge aur sath rahenge beta."*

Never walk with your hand on anyone's shoulder; be the kind of person others lean on. Wherever you find a job, that will be our home, and we will stay together, son.

He remained fragile, and I feared it might be the last time I saw him. His words felt like a weight on my heart. I recall crying the entire night on the train journey to college, especially when the lights were turned off. It was as if all the tears I had held back over the past few months were now pouring out uncontrollably.

Everyone Zigs, You Zag!

Once I reached college, I felt an intense drive coursing through my veins—an urge to challenge fate and claim what should rightfully be mine. Despite feeling wrecked and broken, every fiber of my being burned with a desire to exact revenge on my circumstances.

Driven by this determination, I threw myself into tirelessly exploring ideas, particularly focused on creating the most valuable self-help resource for Indian teenagers. I started working on different models, dedicating months to each one, only to discover their inherent flaws and why they wouldn't succeed.

I preferred sitting in the middle of the row, at the corner seat by the window. It was strategic: not too close to the front where professors might single me out, yet not at the back where they could easily monitor my attentiveness. I immersed myself in books on philosophy, business, religion, psychology—anything that might offer insights into life's complexities. Interestingly, I rarely read these books cover to cover. I skimmed through the main ideas of the books, driven by a desperate quest to uncover the truths about life.

Along the way, I encountered concepts that further fueled my determination, like the idea of "**when everyone zigs, you zag.**"

While others focused on maintaining stellar academic records, I devised my own strategy: "***Do whatever it takes to manifest your vision into reality. It's not about being the top scorer in exams; instead, aim for enough marks to*** *qualify for placements and simultaneously work on creating the changes you want to see in the world."*

Personal Podcast

During the semester, I never actually studied my course material. Instead, I would cram right before exams. I recorded myself explaining important concepts or simply reciting book passages without fully grasping them.

On exam day, I'd wake up at 4 AM, listen to hours of recordings at double speed, and then write down whatever I could recall in the exam. Surprisingly, that strategy paid off.

I didn't face any backs throughout my four years of engineering and achieved a respectable GPA that made me eligible for nearly all the companies during placements. However, those four years were about more than just academics—they were shaped by both my strategy and the twists of fate.

My Raw Emotions

I maintained a steady dialogue with my father about my studies and career plans as part of my strategy to keep him engaged and hopeful. However, despite my efforts, I struggled internally. Anxiety consumed me, filling every waking hour of my day. Anxiety had become so pervasive that I considered it my natural state. I was constantly on edge, making it easy for anything to trigger panic within me.

Over the past year, I had become isolated from my friends, In the first few months of college, I reconnected with a friend from a coaching class I had attended during school. This person was someone I had shared deep and meaningful conversations with in the past. She seem to understand me and despite being geographically distant, she asked for my companionship. I was alone, and thought that I could confide in her, so I said yes.

She was unpredictable—sometimes warm, other times cold. She made me believe that she needs me more than I needed her. But her controlling nature meant she often dismissed my thoughts and feelings.

She didn't understand my anxiety and would mock my struggles and low tolerance for triggers that could lead to panic attacks. My panic responses sometimes led me to react rudely, leaving me feeling embarrassed afterward. I became so frustrated that I would often scream during our calls. Sometimes, late at night, I would go out to an open space, turn off my phone, and scream at the top of my lungs to release my emotions. I felt utterly helpless, unsure how to make things right. The tense situation at home before I left for college kept me in a constant fight-or-flight mode.

Broken, Bullied and Embarrassed

I began to face bullying because of my screaming. I recall one incident vividly: returning to my room during lunch break, only to find it locked from the outside. Panic surged through me, and in my distress, I screamed and knocked on the door frantically.

Unbeknownst to me, it was a deliberate act by others to make the warden hear my screams. The warden eventually arrived, unlocked the door, and offered me quiet comfort without saying a word.

But even so, I felt trapped and powerless. My roommates threatened to complain to the warden and call my home if I raised my voice again. I couldn't risk my father finding out about my struggles; it would devastate him and jeopardize his health. So, I avoided confrontation with them.

However, they took advantage of my silence, escalating their bullying.

They even recorded a video of me showering and circulated it around the hostel. I was crushed, feeling more helpless and anxious than ever before.

Despite the challenges I faced at the hostel—feeling broken, bullied, embarrassed, and helpless—I remained steadfast in pursuing my dreams.

My Second Mother

One day, while seated in class, a professor singled out all the students who appeared unkempt for a group discussion. She had just begun training our class and aimed to help the weakest students improve their speaking skills.

I was the first student she called out, followed by 4-5 others. Initially, she had a certain perception of me based on my casual attire, but by the end of the group discussion, she regarded me as the most outstanding student she had encountered in her career.

She was impressed by the depth of my ideas, my knowledge, and how effectively I articulated them. She commended my calm and composed demeanor in guiding the discussion to a meaningful conclusion.

Despite calling on academically strong students for group discussions, she consistently viewed me as the best among them. She began to believe in me wholeheartedly, but what truly amazed me was how she vocally supported me at every opportunity.

She spoke about me in every class she taught, making me somewhat of a celebrity on campus—a status that initially made me uncomfortable.

Looking back now, I realize how much I needed that support.

Her belief in me, saved me.

She wasn't just a trainer who believed in my abilities; she also made sure I knew she was there for me, much like a second mother, always ready to offer guidance and encouragement whenever I needed it.

Smell the Coffee and Wake Up!

While working on "Awesome Life Geek," I participated in a startup idea competition where I pitched it as a potential social entrepreneurship venture. During the presentation, in front of a full auditorium, one investor bluntly told me to "smell the coffee and wake up to reality."

That day at the competition was crushing. I felt embarrassed and resolved to introspect and return stronger next year. However, the following morning brought an unexpected surprise— "***Awesome Life Geek" had been featured in the Times of India. It was my first appearance in a newspaper ever.***

I called my father, showed him the article, and he was overjoyed. Urmila mam, my mentor and second mother, shared in my happiness and praised how I had proven my critics wrong with this achievement. Following that success, I secured a radio interview at a prestigious journalism college.

The interview focused on my framework designed to complement the education system in India, which was a key aspect of the models I was developing for Awesome Life Geek. I was invited as a guest of honor at their event, and all of this was not only positively influencing my father's health but also boosting my popularity in college. The bullies themselves began questioning their place and future. I had begun to stand out on campus, and in a good way.

The Anti-Suicide Note

My sister informed me about a startup incubated at her IIT campus, that was seeking interns. Despite my initial disbelief, I applied and showcased my work with "Awesome Life Geek." To my surprise, they called me for an interview and offered me accommodation for the entire summer at the IIT campus, along with a stipend to work as a Marketing Strategist. Returning to the campus from which I had been ejected years earlier felt like a surreal victory. I was beginning to gain confidence in myself and my ideas.

However, the shadows of anxiety and the burden of a toxic relationship still weighed heavily on me. I remember recording my voice while crying, pouring out everything that overwhelmed me. I gave that recording to my sister, who had been my shield since my earliest days. I felt deeply broken and alone when she left for her studies back when I was in the ninth standard. I decided to open up to her again, giving her this one chance to save me. This was like, the opposite of what someone might decide to do when they get completely overwhelmed with their life. And this was only possible because I trusted her.

She saved me.

Being the best elder sister one could ask for, she took action to alleviate my suffering. She addressed the basic issues that were weighing on my mind, and this significantly eased my struggles. That summer, she ensured I had a better-performing laptop to work on my ideas. She advocated for the better laptop from my father, who then called me and said, "If you don't ask for better weapons, how do you expect to win the battles?"

To some, this might seem trivial, but for a young immature guy trying to work on his ideas and dreams, while battling through adversity, having such a powerful tool was truly a blessing. A small support can turn into a game changer at that age, people don't understand that.

She encouraged me to talk to her more often when I felt lonely, and she also began filtering what information my parents shared with me. Once again, she resumed her childhood role as a shield between my parents and me. If till date, I close my eyes and think of unconditional love, her face appears before anyone else.

I am second to none!

My last day at that internship was a pivotal moment for me. They threw a party for my farewell, where everyone drank heavily and smoked. To this day, I don't drink or smoke.

As we drove back to the campus, they were all asleep in the car, having spent a lot of money that could have been used for marketing or other productive purposes, instead squandered on alcohol to celebrate the departure of an "intern".

I looked at them and had an epiphany. Deep down, I felt a sense of greater responsibility and maturity compared to them. It dawned on me that the academic institution I attended didn't define my worth.

Even if I had cracked the IIT entrance, I could still have been a failure, and studying at a private institution didn't diminish my potential for success. It was the choices I made that would determine my path, not an exam or a prestigious college. That night, I felt liberated, realizing I was no less capable than those around me.

This revelation sparked an idea to democratize skills and resources for all students, regardless of the academic institution they attended. I envisioned creating a platform where students from various colleges could collaborate on projects. Investors could then discover promising ideas and connect with these student teams to support and develop their concepts further.

Colluding for Innovation

I joined a club run by an alumni and his girlfriend at our college. Their approach involved taking on projects from freelance websites and assigning groups of students to complete them. They encouraged us to share our own ideas so they could assist in developing them.

When I proposed my platform idea to them, they pointed out that it closely aligned with their existing operations. I was taken aback because, to me, what they were doing seemed completely different from my vision. I debated the originality of my idea and managed to negotiate with them to the point where they offered to pay me to develop the same platform for them. Once they offered me money, it solidified my belief in the value of my idea.

I declined their offer, instead turning to a friend who had always supported me in my ventures with "Awesome Life Geek." Together, we decided that we would build a startup of our own. It was an incredible feeling. Over the next few months, we diligently worked on refining our idea and officially registered our company. We conducted extensive market research, reaching out to 3,500 young people to validate our concept.

Reminding to Smell The Coffee

The time for the same startup idea competition arrived, and we returned to the familiar stage. I presented our startup idea, and among the jury members, there was also an IIT professor seated alongside investors, as the chief guest.

In an attempt to gauge our response to tough questions or criticism, he posed a challenge: *"If you truly believed in your idea, why not approach directors of institutions directly instead of targeting students as your consumer base? They could easily get the students on your platform, but being from whichever college you are, you don't have to confidence to go and talk to professors of IITs and NITs because you know, your idea is not worth it."*

I took the mic from my co-founder, and said, *"The discriminatory mindset which you just showcased, is the exact reason I am building this platform for. The students, good at physics, chemistry and maths, are not necessarily better at providing value to society through a business than a guy from a tier 2 or 3 college in India. This platform is about allowing the Indian youth, divided and categorized as "successful" and "failures" so early in their life, to work together without those labels and solve problems for our society and not get limited by the human resource geographically around them."*

This earned me a standing ovation from the students in the crowd. They clapped in support while the professor seemed embarrassed.

Though I didn't win the competition for obviously embarrassing their chief guest, every investor present approached me afterward, offering their business cards and setting up meetings. It was a unique gesture; they didn't extend the same opportunity to any other participant.

One of them mentioned to me that it might not be the best thing to say, but they really liked my response. Sometimes people need to be reminded to "smell the coffee and wake up". Another time, I found myself laughing at the same spot where I had cried a year earlier. And wouldn't you know it, I ended up in the newspaper again the very next day.

We were meeting with investors, and our idea was gaining momentum. The year I had been working towards for the past three years was finally approaching: 2019. The second half of the year would promise either a job or a thriving startup in my grasp. Either way, it was going to be the year I could finally give my father what he had been hoping for all these years.

It was also going to be the year to avenge what had happened in 2016.

I went out with two friends, enjoyed a buffet dinner, and felt genuinely happy. Everything seemed to be going well for me. That night, as I fell asleep, I felt grateful for all that I had achieved through my hard work over the past three years.

No Excuses

When I woke up, I felt a persistent sensation of something poking my eye. Despite washing it several times, the redness persisted along with the discomfort. Concerned, I visited an eye specialist. To my surprise, he asked if I typically experienced back pain in the mornings. I admitted that I did, taken aback by the unexpected question. After conducting several tests, the eye specialist diagnosed me with a disorder triggered by stress.

He explained that the condition, once triggered by my immune system attacking my eye tissues, was incurable. The best I could do was learn to manage it, as it might or might not go into remission over time.

To prevent my immune system from attacking my eye tissues, I was prescribed a course of steroids. The treatment included eye drops that dilated my pupils, causing blurred vision. However, the steroids brought on severe side effects such as extreme aggression, overeating, and restlessness. Over the next few months, I had to endure cycles of taking and then tapering off steroids. During this time, the blurred vision persisted, and when reducing the dosage, I experienced even worse withdrawal symptoms.

At my lowest points, I struggled with overwhelming emotions to the extent that I contemplated jumping off the balcony of my hostel room. It was a difficult period, but in the middle of it all, I found myself engaged in one of the greatest battles of my life.

Fate vs Me

Shortly after the doctor mentioned the possibility of that disorder, he recommended undergoing tests and consulting with other specialists. The prospect of these expenses weighed heavily on my mind. As I left the eye hospital, memories of 2016 came rushing back.

I could see the same pattern repeating itself. This was supposed to be the most pivotal year of my life so far, where I needed to fulfill my father's long-held hopes. Now, faced once again with uncertainty, I couldn't hold back tears as I rode back to the hostel in the auto-rickshaw, worsening my eye condition.

Yet, as I wiped away those tears and stepped out of the auto, a fierce determination overtook me: **no more excuses.**

If fate intended to challenge my spirit, my willpower, my strength, and my burning desire to call my father and say, "The struggle is over, I've made it, now you can rest," then so be it. I was ready to confront whatever destiny had in store for me and defy it if it dared to stand against me.

Considering my father's situation, I made the difficult choice not to disclose my health condition to my family. Instead, I assured them it was a minor infection that would resolve soon. Despite dealing with blurred vision and intense emotions from the steroid treatments, my immediate focus was on securing the funds needed for my tests and treatment.

In addition, the investors we were meeting had emphasized the need for us to generate revenue from our ideas. If I could demonstrate financial viability through my concepts, it would be the ultimate validation as a founder. This would instill trust and potentially secure the seed funding we needed. Determined to pursue both goals simultaneously, I resolved to integrate these two endeavors.

The Secret Coach

Despite the pain and restlessness keeping me awake at night, I channeled my energy into working until 3 or 4 in the morning, brainstorming ways to generate income. I applied for several internships and secured one. During this time, I conceived the idea of offering a micro-learning experience by summarizing 25 non-fiction books and delivering just one page per day via WhatsApp. To enhance engagement, I included creative graphics featuring key book quotes for users to share on social media. To incentivize growth, I introduced a referral program, promising a full refund of the fee if subscribers successfully referred three friends to sign up for the service. I named the service, "The Secret Coach".

Despite my blurred vision, I plunged into research, meticulously summarizing books and crafting daily one-page content, extracting impactful quotes, and designing social media graphics. To manage the distribution, I enlisted the help of a cousin eager for a positive diversion from her research work. She agreed to handle the WhatsApp broadcast list, receiving weekly content in advance.

With everything set, I composed a compelling message to attract subscribers. I highlighted my achievements over the past year and pitched the opportunity for them to read 25 books in 25 weeks and make the remaining year productive, all for just Rs. 199. The response exceeded my expectations: in just 1.5 weeks, I secured enough direct and referral sign-ups to raise approximately Rs. 10,000.

Going GAGA Over This!

Despite my challenges—swollen face, messed up emotional state especially the aggression inside my chest, erratic diet, and persistent blurred vision—I managed to gather enough money for my tests and doctor visits.

With determination, I headed to the office of a potential investor who owned a prestigious co-working space in the city. He had been giving me regular meetings every other week. I proudly disclosed that I had earned Rs. 10,000 as requested by him, to show earnings through my ideas.

To validate my claim, he asked to see my passbook. After verifying the details, he was genuinely impressed with what I had achieved. He said, ***"Suyash, I am going GAGA over this, right now!"***.

He offered me free access to his premium co-working space and scheduled a weekly one-hour meeting to kickstart my startup journey. He assured me of covering expenses as necessary but emphasized the importance of regular updates on our progress.

Leaving his office, I had a cup of chai, sitting alone at the side of the road just downstairs. I felt like an injured lion—proud and determined. That day, I earned my own respect. I knew deep down that I am a tough soul; my fate couldn't defeat me.

Choosing My Battles

The tests revealed that I was in the early stages of the condition, and with proper self-care, there was a chance I could push the disease into remission, though nothing was guaranteed.

This battle would have to wait; right now, my priority was restoring my vision to make this year everything it was meant to be.

The steroids had taken a toll, leaving me weak. I needed daily injections of essential vitamins to support my nervous system and prevent collapse. Despite these challenges, I continued to show up at college every day, walking into rooms ready to conquer whatever lay ahead. During our mock placement preparations, despite my altered health, I continued to excel and secure top positions. Some began to envy me because even at my lowest, they couldn't surpass me. Not just envy, but to some, I inadvertently sparked admiration and inspiration as well.

Reflecting on the strength it took to remain undefeated still gives me goosebumps.

The workload I was managing with my compromised health was becoming overwhelming. Balancing the demands of building a startup while also preparing for job placements created a significant conflict. Although my health was improving slightly, the pressure of impending job interviews added to the stress.

On a sunny Sunday afternoon, I decided to take a break and get a glass of chai, determined to make a decision about my next steps. It was then that my father called. In the course of our conversation, he expressed how much he wished my sister and I were there with him in that moment.

In that emotional moment, my father shared his health concerns and his deep desire for us to be closer together. He abruptly ended the call, likely to conceal his tears, only to call back later and reassure me that everything was fine and to focus on my career.

Despite his attempt to lighten the mood, his heartfelt words had already given me the clarity I needed.

I realized that I couldn't jeopardize my father's hopes by dedicating my time and energy to my startup at this moment.

Given my past experiences, failure was not an option I could afford.

It became clear to me that I needed to set aside my idea for now and focus on getting established to alleviate his worries about our family's future. So, I made the difficult decision to shut down the company. Despite having applied to several VC funding opportunities.

I recall receiving a call during the second last semester exams. The VC informed us that we had been selected as one of the top 3 promising startups in India vying for their funding. They required us to be in Delhi within the next 2 days to compete for the final funding against the other two startups.

But going there, would mean missing at least one of my semester exam. A back would risk my chances of eligible candidature in companies for placement.

As I hung up the phone, I couldn't shake the image of my father's face from my mind. I closed my eyes, envisioned the phone call I had longed to make for the past four years, telling him that our struggle was finally over.

With a heavy heart, I sighed and let go of that opportunity.

4-Minute 33-Second

After the exams concluded, a few companies visited our college, but my academic standing prevented me from being eligible for those opportunities. Now that my vision had fully returned, I had limited time to prepare for upcoming interviews. I focused on revising technical concepts and practicing technical questions rigorously to ensure I could perform well in the majority of the placement drives.

As I traveled home on the train, I received an email about a third company visiting our campus. This company was offering two roles. Although the email didn't specify the compensation, the second job description resonated with my career aspirations, affirming that this was the path I wanted to pursue in life.

Immediate Probability vs Long-Term Alignment

The situation became tricky: I had only 10 days to prepare for the technical concepts needed for the upcoming companies visiting campus one after another. Simultaneously, I needed to ready myself to compete for the role offered by the third company, where I would be up against MBA students who naturally had an edge. Balancing preparation time between technical interviews and competing for the desired role became crucial.

I faced a dilemma. I could either give my best effort for the role that truly resonated with me, knowing it aligned with my values and authenticity, or spread my efforts across multiple roles to increase my chances of securing any job. Opting for the latter would likely improve my probability of success, but the potential reward of pursuing what felt right for me personally and professionally would be greater in the former option. It was a decision between immediate probability versus long-term alignment with my values and aspirations

I made up my mind to go all-in for this one job opportunity.

Large Frog in the Room at 2AM

I sat down and meticulously researched, crafting a 10-day plan to prepare for the upcoming placement drive. It reminded me of the intensive planning I used to do for the JEE exams three years ago. This was my final chance to make it count. My plan factored in time for traveling back to college, allowing myself five hours of sleep each night, and dedicating every waking hour to training and preparing for the interview process.

During those 10 days, I intentionally cut off all my connections. I isolated myself from friends and acquaintances, avoiding any distractions or discussions about what I was focusing on. I made sure not to seek advice or opinions from anyone to maintain my singular focus and prevent outside influences.

I recall being completely immersed in my preparations. On the third-to-last day, around 2 am, after completing my tasks for the day, I was startled to find a large frog sitting near my bed in my room. It was a terrifying sight, and I couldn't fathom how it had gotten in or how long it had been there. I was so focused at making these 10 days work, that I had lost eyes and ears for anything else happening in my surrounding.

I proceeded with my first test. I opted for the city where my companion lived as my preferred job location. Such was the precision of my preparation that I felt confident I would perform well in the test. So, I proceeded with my preparations for the interviews that would follow as scheduled.

The evening before the interviews, amidst heavy rain, we received the final list of students who had qualified from among approximately 3000 candidates. Seeing my name on that list was a moment of validation. I had some last-minute errands to run, including printing necessary documents and picking up a new shirt for the interviews. The weight gain from the steroids had caused my old uniform to no longer fit properly, adding to the urgency of the situation.

Despite the challenges, I braved the storm to get a haircut and print out necessary documents. However, my new shirt wasn't ready in time for the interviews. I had no choice but to wear the old shirt that very evidently no longer fit me well.

Initially embarrassed and tensed about my impression, I looked myself in the mirror and firmly said, ***"Suyash, no excuses. You can't let your fate dictate this moment. You've got this!"***

You Have 30 Seconds to Change My Mind

I arrived at the interview location in my friend's car, throughout the journey, I continued listening to my own recorded voice at double speed, reviewing my resume and anticipating potential interview questions. I also brushed up on demographic data to better handle guesstimate questions.

During the case study round, a professor approached and inquired about the difficulty level of the case given. Without hesitation, I confidently exclaimed, "It's easy!" It was then that I noticed the entire group of students in the room looking at me. It dawned on me that what seemed straightforward to me might not be the case for everyone else.

Now, in the first round of interviews, we were expected to answer questions based on the case study we had analyzed. As I waited for my turn, others approached me, seeking answers and explanations for the case study. I won't deny that it was difficult for me to refuse anyone seeking my help.

Nonetheless, I stood my ground and said no, even to friends I had known for a long time. That day was dedicated to my father, not just my personal ambitions.

I successfully passed the first round of interviews, but in the second round, there was a tense moment when the interviewer threw my resume on the table and bluntly stated, "I don't think you're suited for the job." There was a moment of silence, during which I remained calm and composed.

After what felt like an eternity, the interviewer spoke again. **"Okay, you have 30 seconds to change my mind,"** he said.

I reverted to the initial step I took during my preparation: mapping my values with the company's values. Over the past three years, I had dedicated myself to living and working in alignment with my own values and principles.

Drawing from this experience, I provided concrete examples from my college years that demonstrated how closely I aligned with the core values of their organization. This approach stunned and resonated well with the interviewer, and I advanced to the final round of the selection process.

In the final round of the interview, the atmosphere was intentionally relaxed to see if I would slip up. However, because of my thorough preparation, I maintained the same composed demeanor as in the previous three rounds of evaluations.

Now, all that was left was to wait for the results.

The Phone Call

As evening approached and I walked down the corridor, I found myself praying to Shiva— *"**Mahadev, bless me today, not for myself, but for my father's sake**"*. They gathered us in the waiting room to announce the results.

When they called my name, tears welled up in my eyes. After the group photo, as I left the room, my legs shook and my hands trembled. I quickly switched on the call recorder and dialed Papa's number.

"Papa, I got placed," I said through tears. "Arey Waah, Arey Waah Beta, Sanyam Banae Rakhna, Tumne Dila Die Hamein Beta" he exclaimed joyfully.

(Wow son, maintain your composure, you have given me what I longed for)

That 4-minute 33-second phone call recording will always be the greatest achievement of my life.

I Will Reponsible!

Six months later, when I arrived at my job location, I decided to surprise my long-distance companion whom I had been with for the past three years. Despite the conflicts we had endured, I had always made an effort to support her throughout those years.

I thought to myself, "***This is it! Everything is finally aligned. I've achieved what I've been chasing after. Now is the time to relax and spend quality time with the people I cherish.***"

If anyone was left most surprised by the surprise visit, it was me. I discovered that she had been cheating on me with multiple people over the past three years. This shattered me. I walked out of her life by congratulating her on the castle of lies she had built, and never looked back.

I felt like a fool, and those close to me didn't hold back their opinions about my naivety either. Processing the betrayal was incredibly difficult. Once again, I retreated into myself and set a strict timeline: one month to completely heal from the experience. I made a pact with myself—I allowed 15 days to grieve and feel the pain, and then for the next 15 days, I committed to actively redirecting my thoughts whenever they drifted to her or what had happened.

It's Her Choice

I had to come to terms with the fact that I couldn't control other people's decisions; they are the ultimate decision-makers of their own lives. If she chose to act in a certain way, it was her choice, and there was nothing I could do to change that. Although I was responsible for my own behavior as well. Instead of focusing on her actions, I redirected my attention to my own behavior and actions. I reflected on that a lot and committed myself to improving myself and becoming more emotionally intelligent.

Learning from that experience brought a profound calmness to my behavior.

From that moment onward, I understood that everyone is the ultimate decision-maker for themselves, and I could never expect them to act a certain way. Instead, I focused on how I treated others, ensuring my behavior always reflected my values, no matter how chaotic the situation. This shift in perspective changed me forever. I asked myself if I would ever betray someone's trust or dedication in the same way, and the answer was a resounding no. This realization defined me and became my guiding principle as I moved forward. I needed to carry this understanding firmly in my mind as I walked away.

Cricket, Politics and Life

I recovered from that setback more swiftly than I anticipated. Then, the COVID-19 pandemic swept across the world. Initially, I was confined with my flatmates for a couple of months due to travel restrictions. Eventually, I managed to return home.

My job kept me occupied for most of the time, but whatever free moments I had, I dedicated them to spending quality time with my parents. I even discussed my sister's marriage with my father and shared details about my jiju, my brother-in-law and the next month, my sister got married. Due to his health complications and the risks associated with COVID, my father couldn't attend the ceremony. Throughout the event, he was constantly on the phone with me. Both of us were emotional, often in tears.

I felt the weight of trying to fill my father's shoes, knowing how deeply he wished to be present for his daughter's wedding. His absence weighed heavily on him, and it was a poignant reminder of his love and dedication as a father.

My father and I had a cherished routine of discussing my office experiences while he shared stories from his life. Our conversations were a delightful mix of cricket, politics, and business, always filled with his wisdom and anecdotes. He loved to share his stories, but I loved listening to them even more. Those moments were a treasure trove of connection and learning, and they brought us closer in a way that I will always hold dear. Especially whenever he found that we aligned on certain values behind my decisions. He looked happy that I was living my life with a similar mindset as him. . However, I started noticing that he was becoming weaker.

Don't Tell Anyone

He had been managing his medications independently, since forever. It never occurred to us that he might be wrong in doing so as well. He was so exhausted from all the surgeries and different kinds of experiences at different hospitals that gradually he just started taking care of every medical need of his, on his own.

One day, he nearly fainted, prompting us to discover that his sugar levels were dangerously low. It turned out he had been taking sugar medication without a proper diagnosis. We had several arguments about it.

It came to light that after his last surgery, the doctor had instructed him to avoid sugar to prevent infections during recovery. However, he wasn't thinking clearly due to anxiety and was taking not just sugar medication, but various other medicines without proper diagnosis.

His hypoglycemic attacks became more frequent, yet he refused to listen to our advice. I remember it was my mother's birthday. My sister, visiting home at the time, baked a cake for her. As my mother cut the cake, my father suffered another hypoglycemic attack. I checked his sugar levels and they were dangerously low. I looked at him with a mix of hurt and tears in my eyes.

He pleaded with me not to tell anyone else at home.

This continued for a couple of months, until one day when he was sitting on his bed, staring outside the room lost in thought. As I observed him, a deep realization dawned on me.

I Need to Take Charge

I realized that I need to take care of him. And for that, I need to take charge.

I approached him and insisted that we get all his tests done. I mentioned that my company sponsors these tests quarterly, and it would be a waste not to take advantage of it. He agreed, saying, "Okay, then save it for when I'll be getting my last surgery done in the next couple of months. I feel I'll be able to walk properly after that." That night, I cried deeply.

I couldn't bring myself to believe that he would endure another surgery. It became clear to me that I needed to do everything in my power to assist him;

This was the very purpose behind everything I had strived for since childhood.

I said to him, "Hey, I checked and we can get those tests done again during your surgery because they will be covered by insurance. Let's get this one done now. It will be a full body test, and I've already booked it for this coming Wednesday. We have three days until then, so you can manage your medications in a way that won't affect the test results."

He scolded me a bit for not asking before booking it, but I didn't mind because I felt it was important to take charge and make things right.

It was Tuesday evening, during one of my office meetings on Zoom, when I heard him screaming from the washroom. My mom rushed to him, and after some time, she managed to bring him out. He couldn't walk on his own, so I helped him and got him onto the bed. He said he was feeling extremely weak and couldn't walk. Convinced he had COVID, I immediately searched and explained the symptoms to him, reassuring him it wasn't COVID.

I urged him to see a doctor, but he refused. I called my friend, who's more like a brother to me now, and asked him to be ready in case we needed to take my father to the hospital. The next day, the samples were collected for the test I had booked. My father insisted on waiting for the results. He could only walk with the support of my mother or me.

Meanwhile, my job was demanding and didn't allow me even an hour to gather my thoughts. Being new to the job, I struggled to understand what was acceptable and what wasn't. In the midst of a toxic and hectic workday, I called my friend again.

Despite knowing that my father suspected he had COVID, my friend immediately showed up at my house. It's a moment I'll never forget.

We went together to buy a wheelchair on his bike and brought it home. When I showed it to my father, he hugged me and shed a few tears. I tried to stay strong. I said to him, "Please trust me. Once your reports come, let's go to the hospital."

He said, "No, let's first show it to my doctor friends." We followed his suggestion, but his friend barely glanced at the reports and casually remarked, "I don't think he can survive. You should keep him at home and take care of him."

I was deeply offended by his insensitive comment. Snatching the report back, I returned home and firmly told my father, "I'm going out to find a good hospital for you."

Trust Me, If Anything Happens, I Will Be Responsible!

As I prepared to leave with my friend to find a hospital for him, my father said to my mother, "*If my son wants it so badly for me to live, then I want to live too.*"

I struggled to hold back my tears. After hours of searching and consulting with others, I managed to arrange for his admission the next day. Returning home, I shared the news with him.

The next morning, he told me that if I took him to the hospital, he wouldn't come back alive. I set down my cup of chai on the table and, brimming with a love, courage and determination that I had never felt so strongly before, I looked him straight in the eyes and said, "*You have to trust me. I will never let anything happen to you. If anything happens, I will be responsible. Just trust me."*

I got him admitted, all the while continuing to send work deliverables to my office, managing my father's business from home, arranging food for them, and ensuring my mother could focus on being with him. I also hired a personal nurse to assist with his care, relieving my mother of some of the burden. Over the years, she had sacrificed her life completely to my father and our family's well-being. Now, I was using my own money and resolutely ignoring any advice on how to handle the situation.

I simply couldn't bear to see either of them suffer any longer.

In the hospital, after undergoing blood transfusions and a few other treatments in just the first two days, he began to feel a bit better. He was even joking around. It was on the second day when I visited him that he shared a story about how he selectively forwards WhatsApp messages to certain people and joked about how everyone notices if he skips sending those good morning texts. He showed me my sister's WhatsApp display picture and commented on how my sister, her husband, and their dog looked great together. I felt a bit relieved when I left the hospital that day.

Everything that Matters to You

The next day, however, my mother called and told me that my father was not doing well at all. He had diarrhea and had taken medication to stop it on his own, but now he was not fully conscious. I rushed to the hospital and found that my father was not responding normally at all. He seemed to be only half awake, which greatly concerned my mother, who started crying. I quickly booked a cab for her to go home, and the doctors informed me that his condition had worsened, and they needed to shift him to the ICU.

He also mentioned that there might be a possibility that we may not be able to save him. My heart sank, and I struggled to hold back my tears, keeping this dialogue internalized.

I immediately instructed my mom to stay at home, sent off the final deliverable of the month at my office with the message that I would be unavailable for a few days because my father was in ICU. Gathering some sheets, I resolved to stay by his side in the hospital.

When he regained consciousness the next day, I approached him and attempted to engage him in conversation.

To my dismay, he didn't recognize me.

I was looking at him in the eye, he was trying to recognize me, he started guessing names of my elder cousins. For a moment, it felt like, time had stopped for me. He kept guessing, and I was looking at him, feeling abandoned. I kept this heart-wrenching development to myself.

Inhaled as much courage as I could, and exhaled the heaviness because the situation needed my full attention. I could not afford being vulnerable at the moment, it could cost him his life.

The doctors recommended conducting several brain tests, which we promptly arranged. Throughout this period, he remained conscious. Once the reports of the brain tests were available, I spared no effort in consulting every reputable hospital and doctor in my city, going alone with his reports for each consultation.

Everyone agreed it was a challenging situation. Some expressed doubts about his recovery. One doctor went as far as suggesting he seemed depressed and lacked the will to live. This startled me, and I almost challenged him. How could he make such a diagnosis based on the medical reports alone? I mean, what are the markers for it? It made no sense to me.

Cookies?

I entered the ICU to find him sleeping. The doctors delivered grim news: his vitals were deteriorating, and his platelet count was dropping.

Despite the seriousness of the situation, I found myself inundated with calls from a distant relative known for being pathetic. I chose not to answer any of them. I faced criticism from everyone around me, insisting that I should take the calls, as they believed they had a stake in my father's situation too. Reluctantly, I decided to speak with them. They urged me to bring my father to their city and get him admitted to PGI (Post Graduate Institute of Medical

Education and Research). I explained that despite efforts from my contacts, admission to PGI was challenging due to the COVID-19 pandemic. They assured me that they could handle it and insisted I bring him to their city. They insisted their local connections and influence would be useful.

I arranged for the best ambulance in town and we embarked on a risky 6-7 hour journey to reach PGI. Throughout the trip, my father remained unconscious, but whenever I called out to him, he would turn his head toward me, even with his eyes closed. That simple gesture of acknowledgment was the only hope keeping me going.

When we arrived, I stepped out of the ambulance and encountered the son of my father's close relative.

He offered me cookies, but I declined. Then he asked, "So, what's the plan?"

I was taken aback and replied, "What plan?" He suggested we go talk to the hospital staff to get my father admitted. I hesitated, reminding him of his earlier claim about having connections. I explained that even with my own efforts, the hospital wasn't admitting patients due to the COVID outbreak. Despite my reservations, he insisted we try.

We approached the reception, but they declined to admit him. I was utterly disgusted by the audacity of the people I was dealing with. My father was in a coma like state in that ambulance, we had travelled for hours to come here, because they had insisted and assured us, and standing here, he was offering cookies and asking what is the plan? The problem was not they could not get us admitted, the problem was that they had so casually asked us to come here risking my father's life without any serious thought.

Fuming with anger, I distanced myself from them and frantically searched for nearby hospitals on Google. There was a private hospital just 10 kilometers away, but the ambulance driver demanded an exorbitant fee for the change in plans. Feeling helpless, I reluctantly agreed to the extra charges.

Counted on My Fingers

After reaching the private hospital, I learned they permitted only one person inside. I decided to go in myself. My father lay on a stretcher in the hospital hallway while I stood at the reception, my mind racing with the grim news from the staff.

They informed me that while they could attempt treatment, they believed he wouldn't survive.

They presented the staggering costs of care, amounting to lakhs per day. They urged me to take my time in making a decision. Without hesitation, I called my mother. I asked her for the exact amount of savings she and Papa had.

She gave me a number, and in that moment, I calculated how many days we could afford to keep him in the hospital if we spent every rupee they had saved and every rupee I had earned up to that point.

I returned to the reception and said, "Yes, admit him right now." They handed me forms to sign, stating that I had been informed about my father's critical condition and that they wouldn't be held responsible if he passed away.

They also showed me the severe bed sores he had developed because the hospital in my hometown had not taken proper care of him. They ensured he was comfortable, placing him in an extremely premium facility and hooking him up to a ventilator in their ICU.

Despite all the turmoil, I felt a sense of relief seeing him being cared for by the best professionals available. The environment was pristine, premium, and the doctors appeared genuinely dedicated to his well-being.

I had to receive updates from them daily, and each time I came out, I would tell everyone that he was stable and improving, although the doctors cautioned me not to get too hopeful.

They would actually inform me about additional health issues he was facing every day. On the third day, I had to arrange for approximately 6 units of blood and a few units of plasma for him. In an unfamiliar city, I managed to arrange for 10 units of blood, partly through a social media post seeking donors.

An old friend who had called my mother's number—perhaps from our school days when I didn't have my own phone—learned about our situation. He consoled my mother and assured her that if I couldn't arrange enough blood, he and his brother along with a few friends would fly down to donate. When my mother shared this with me, that phone call turned our friendship into a lifelong brotherhood.

Nahi Rahe

The day I arranged the blood, in the briefing that day, the doctor reiterated the same grim prognosis. But within me, something shifted. The fire that had sustained me was flickering. I felt an inexplicable heaviness in my heart.

During my authorized visit to the ICU, I walked in and stood by his side. "Papa, I am here," I said softly.

His pulse seemed to respond. Tears welled up in my eyes. I knew he could hear me.

"I will take care of everything that mattered to you. I promise to take care of everything. Don't worry, I will always take care of everything."

Those were the only words I could manage, because any more and I would break down completely.

I walked away, returning to the room I had rented near the hospital. That night, my cousin brother, who had been an immense support throughout this ordeal, and a few other close relatives from my mother's side—who had always stood by my father—were staying near the hospital.

I was utterly exhausted from arranging all the blood donations. I called my mother, who was staying at our local relatives' house, and asked her not to send dinner for me.

Deep down, my soul knew something that my mind wasn't ready to acknowledge or articulate.

I received a call at 3:30 AM from my uncle (mama ji), urgently asking me to come to the hospital. Without hesitation, I sprinted from my hotel towards the hospital. Even as I rushed there, deep inside, my soul seemed to grasp what was about to happen. Yet, my heart and mind were still grappling with the enormity of the situation.

Arriving at the hospital gates, my uncle directed me to sit in his car parked across the road.

Another close relative, whom I affectionately called Nanu, and who shared a deep bond with my father, sat on the passenger seat of the car opposite me. He appeared somewhat inebriated, tears streaming down his face.

Looking directly into my eyes, he uttered, "NAHI RAHE" ("HE IS NO MORE"). As he began to sob, he continued, "TUMHE SABKO SMBHALNA HAI, SMBHALO PEHLE KHUD KO" ("YOU HAVE TO TAKE CARE OF EVERYONE, TAKE CARE OF YOURSELF FIRST").

Ultimate Endpoint of Love

I was shaking uncontrollably and tears poured down my face, but with a deep breath, I managed to hold back the rest.

Inhaling deeply, I summoned courage I never knew I had. I stopped crying, though my hands continued to tremble.

I asked him if my mom or sister knew. They said no, only I knew. They added that a local relative had been called to bring my father's clothes, so my mother would soon find out. I needed to go inside the hospital with the clothes as they were calling me for formalities. I walked into the hospital, with that relative following closely behind me.

Alone, I entered the ICU facility where a form awaited me. It detailed the circumstances of how and when the dearest man, whose happiness I had dedicated my life to up until this point, had passed away.

As I signed, I struggled to steady my trembling hands, as though the calmness of my hands could quell the storm that had engulfed my family.

Slowly, I made my way to the room where he lay, covered in a white sheet.

Through tear-filled eyes, I glimpsed the ultimate endpoint of love.

There he lay, yet he wasn't truly there anymore. Despite my overflowing love for him, he could no longer feel any of it. How was this possible? How could he simply cease to exist? Exiting the ICU, my mind was blank.

Each passing moment felt like a fresh wound etching itself into my raw soul.

They requested me to settle the final bills. In that moment, I recalled a conversation with my father about the starting bonus from my job. My mother jokingly suggested giving it all to him, to which I replied that everything I had was already his. He smiled and said, "Keep it safe." I used my card to pay the bonus amount, settling the bills and obtaining the clearance receipt for my father's body.

I called my Jiju and shared the news with him, asking him to inform my sister, because I trusted that he would be able to support her. During the 6-hour journey back to my hometown in the ambulance, holding his phone alongside mine, I felt like I now carried his responsibilities in my hands. I called everyone in his contacts to deliver the news. Despite repeating endlessly that he was gone, it still felt unreal to me.

Warmth of Tears

We arrived home, and I held back my tears in front of my mother and sister. But during his final journey from our home to the cremation site, I screamed at the top of my lungs on the streets of Banaras. It was a harrowing and surreal experience.

The only warmth I could feel in those moments was of my own tears running down my face. My voice still echoes in my mind whenever I walk down those roads. It's as if the streets, trees, air, and buildings couldn't contain my pain and continue to spill it to this day.

As I gave Agni to his Chita and stood a few steps away, watching the fire begin to consume the one we believed belonged to us and us alone for our entire lives, I felt my world changing forever. He was slipping away from me.

My protector, my guiding light, my pole star, my idol—the one whose acceptance and appreciation I had sought in everything I did in my life. All the people who had accompanied him on his final journey stood in small groups of two or three.

The darkness around us was illuminated by the flickering flames on the ghat, casting a somber glow over the Ganges river beyond.

Fortitude Forever

For the next few months, our family endured the toughest challenges we had ever faced. I fell ill with Dengue, and shortly after, all of us contracted COVID-19. It felt as though something was determined to extinguish any remaining hope and vitality within us.

Surviving my workplace during that time was daunting. ***Balancing overwhelming workloads while grieving and explaining myself needlessly felt like defending a lifeless body from vultures.***

To compound matters, my health disorder, which had previously affected my eyes, resurfaced. This time, it also brought severe back pain, reaching a point where I struggled to even lift a water bottle.

Chasing that 1% Chance

Emotionally, I sank to my lowest point. Despite my own struggles, I assured my sister that everything was under control and encouraged her to pursue her plans abroad. Witnessing my mother's solitude and occasional tears was unbearable, so I made a concerted effort to maintain a cheerful attitude around her. I involved her in every little thing or activity to bring a smile to her face.

I used to feel overwhelmed every day. I sat down one day with a strong urge to end my life, but instead, I picked up a pen and paper.

I divided the paper with a margin in the middle. On the left side, I wrote "D" for "What if I choose to Die," and on the right, I wrote "L" for "What if I choose to Live." I listed 4-5 things that mattered most to me in life. Under "D" for each of them, I wrote, "Will definitely fail at this and it will have no chance of ever turning into a positive thing." On the right side under "L," I wrote, "*There is just a 1% chance maybe of this thing actually working out in my favor.*"

This was one of the most powerful things I have ever done in my life.

As I looked at the page, it became clear: if I give up, I will 100% fail at everything that matters to me. But if I choose to live and fight with all I have, there's a 1% chance I can turn my life around. I cried. And in that moment, I made a decision—I would chase that 1% with everything I had in me!

I began approaching everything in my life with a singular focus: chasing that 1% chance.

I hired a trainer to help manage my disorder and aimed to push it into remission through exercise. At work, I tackled my responsibilities with renewed sincerity and motivation. I continued to support my family without ever asking for anything in return or voicing any complaints. I gave my all.

Years of battling like this, brought few victories. The most significant triumph was seeing our mother's happiness, thanks to my sister's and my relentless efforts. My career had also shown remarkable growth, exceeding my expectations. Additionally, through my imperfect yet unwavering dedication, and my trainer's expertise, my disorder went into remission!

From the point where I couldn't even lift a water bottle, I was easily completing 20 pushups in one go.

Looking Fate in The Eyes

And yet a few heart crushing losses made my life seemingly collapsing like a house of cards, I found myself sinking into deep depression. Getting out of bed in the morning became an immense struggle each day. I had my reasons to feel this way.

It took me an hour and a half each morning just to muster the courage to get out of bed and confront my life. It felt as though everything I had built over these years, the way I had risen from the ashes, was temporary, and ultimately, I had failed at life.

For a couple of months, I felt like I was spiraling down, finally hitting rock bottom. During that darkest period, I had a profound realization:

Since life kept throwing fights my way, one after another, I realized I didn't have the option to feel broken.

Expecting a specific outcome wasn't serving me anymore. So, I made a crucial decision: I would truly save myself. I would challenge my fate and stare it down instead of fearing it.

This determination to confront my destiny head-on, without fear, became the core of my identity.

Adopting this new identity gave me a renewed sense of purpose. I chose to become a warrior for life, not fixated on outcomes but committed to the battle itself.

This shift in understanding transformed me from someone obsessed with having an "awesome life" into a person who truly embodies "Fortitude Forever."

I stopped measuring my worth by external achievements or outcomes and instead focused on my unwavering determination to face whatever came my way with courage and strength.

Instilling The Warrior Mindset

Through this book, I am not promising you immense wealth or fame through a collection of life hacks. Instead, I want to share with you a mindset, deeply rooted in both psychological research and philosophical perspectives, that has transformed me into a warrior.

Regardless of the outcomes, irrespective of what life hurls my way, no matter how many times I falter or the missteps I take: I keep fighting.

This mindset is about having resilience, finding strength within adversity, and viewing each setback as another epoch in your epic journey rather than a defeat. It's about cultivating an indomitable spirit that remains steadfast in the face of hardship.

If I can instill this mindset in you, I assure you that you will achieve far more than if you were to surrender when confronted with life's inevitable challenges.

I want you to experience the power of relentless perseverance, the courage to confront your deepest fears, and the fortitude to rise again and again. My aspiration is to inspire you to become a warrior in your own life, ready to confront whatever comes your way with unwavering confidence and unyielding tenacity.

Let this book transform you, fortify you, and elevate your courage to heights you never imagined possible.

Section II

1. Should I Give Up?

The worst nightmares are born from the most sought-after dreams.

I will start again, with the same words as in the beginning of this book.

Your heart is bruised and battered. You might be exhausted from pouring all your energy and soul into crafting beautiful memories, only to watch them crumble into painful experiences. Life is meant to have its highs and lows, but why do you always end up sifting through the ashes of your most cherished and foundational dreams? It feels like some unseen force is relentlessly trying to bring you to your knees, urging you to give up and abandon your dreams. It's not just the isolated failures, but the relentless pattern of heartbreak that makes you want to stop trying. No one's advice seems to resonate because it feels like no one has faced as many defeats as you have.

I feel your pain, deeply.

I'll be honest with you. I haven't found the light at the end of this tunnel either. I don't even know if it exists. I, too, feel the weight of this exhaustion.

So, should we give up?

NO.

I look fate in the eyes and say, "I don't deserve this. Even if everyone and everything I ever loved abandoned me, I

will not join them in this contempt. I will never abandon myself."

You once had dreams, giving up on your dreams is giving up on a part of yourself. Fighting back is a way of honoring your true self and your deepest desires. It's about staying true to who you are and what you believe in, no matter how difficult the journey may be. I strongly believe in this. And if in the end, I don't get what I deserve, at least I fought with everything I had. I didn't give up on myself, and that act of defiance is a victory in itself. If not anything, at least I deserve that victory, and I will claim it.

The dreams that fill our hearts with hope and purpose are the same ones that, when unfulfilled, leave us shattered. This paradox is at the core of the human experience. We dream because we see the potential for joy and fulfillment, yet it is this very pursuit that exposes us to profound pain. The higher we aim, the harder we fall. It's a cruel irony that the same dreams that give our lives meaning can also be the source of our greatest anguish.

Yet, in this paradox lies the essence of fortitude. The capacity to dream, to strive, and to endure the inevitable disappointments is what makes us resilient. It is this relentless pursuit, despite the risk of heartbreak, that defines our strength.

Your notion of success centers around tangible achievements—reaching a goal, obtaining a certain status, or acquiring material wealth. You need to recognize that the ultimate victory lies in the pursuit itself. It is in the courage to chase our dreams, the resilience to withstand setbacks, and the integrity to stay true to our values. It is in the growth, the learning, and the fulfillment we find along the way. Life is a continuous journey with no definitive endpoint but death. And till your last breath, the pursuit of your dreams is a process, filled with moments of joy, hardship, and everything in between. By embracing this process, we shift our focus from a distant end goal to the present moment. The process of striving, struggling, and enduring shapes us in profound ways.

In embracing this perspective, we find the strength to carry on. The act of striving, even in the face of repeated failure, becomes a testament to our character. Each setback is an opportunity for growth, a chance to learn more about ourselves and the world around us. It is through this ongoing journey that we build resilience, develop deeper self-awareness, and cultivate a profound sense of purpose.

Psychologically, this approach aligns with the concept of growth mindset, as introduced by psychologist Carol Dweck. A growth mindset is the belief that abilities and intelligence can be developed through dedication and hard work. This perspective encourages a love of learning and resilience, essential traits for overcoming adversity. Instead of viewing failures as a reflection of your inherent abilities, see them as opportunities to grow and improve. This shift in mindset can transform your approach to challenges, making you more adaptable and persistent in the face of obstacles. We will talk about this again, later in this book.

Existentialists like Jean-Paul Sartre and Friedrich Nietzsche explored the inherent meaninglessness of life and the freedom we have to create our own meaning. In the face of a seemingly indifferent universe, it is our responsibility to find purpose and meaning through our actions and choices. This perspective empowers us to take ownership of our lives and to see the pursuit of our dreams as a fundamental part of our existence. It's not about the outcome, but about the act of creating and living authentically.

Philosophically, this journey also deeply echoes the teachings of Stoicism. Stoic philosophers like Epictetus and Marcus Aurelius emphasized the importance of focusing on what we can control and accepting what we cannot. According to Stoicism, we cannot control the external events in our lives, but we can control our responses to them. This philosophy teaches us to embrace the process and find peace in the effort, regardless of the outcome. It's about finding strength within, and understanding that true success lies in our inner virtue and integrity, not in external achievements. Again, stoic philosophy will be revisited multiple times in this book, and for the right reasons.

Radical acceptance is a core concept in dialectical behavior therapy (DBT), a therapeutic approach developed by Dr. Marsha Linehan. It involves fully and wholeheartedly accepting your current reality without judgment, resistance, or denial. This acceptance is not about approving or liking the situation but about recognizing and acknowledging it as it is. By embracing radical acceptance, individuals can free themselves from the emotional burden of resistance and focus their energy on addressing and navigating their circumstances effectively.

Accept that the battle has begun, and focus your energy on fighting it.

Radical acceptance is crucial because it addresses the fundamental human tendency to resist and deny painful experiences. This resistance often leads to increased suffering, as it compounds the original pain with additional layers of frustration, anger, and hopelessness. By practicing radical acceptance, individuals can break this cycle and create space for healing and growth. The first step in practicing radical acceptance is to acknowledge the pain and disappointment you are experiencing. This involves recognizing the reality of the situation and the emotions it evokes. For instance, if you have experienced a significant loss, radical acceptance means allowing yourself to feel the grief and sadness fully, rather than trying to suppress or ignore these emotions.

Once you have acknowledged your pain, the next step is to let go of judgment. This means refraining from labeling your emotions as good or bad, or yourself as weak or strong for feeling them. Instead, view your emotions as natural responses to your circumstances. By removing judgment, you reduce the additional emotional burden that comes from self-criticism and societal expectations.

When you accept reality as it is, you reduce the emotional suffering caused by resistance. Instead of expending energy on fighting against the past (what you cannot change), you can focus on coping with and adapting to your situation to put up a good fight for your future (on which you still have influence on). This shift in perspective can alleviate feelings of frustration and helplessness.

Radical acceptance enhances emotional regulation by promoting mindfulness and present-moment awareness. By accepting your emotions without judgment, you become better equipped to manage and respond to them constructively. This increased emotional regulation can lead to improved mental health and well-being. Radical acceptance paves way for resilience by helping individuals adapt to and navigate challenging situations. When you accept reality, you can develop a clearer understanding of your circumstances and identify practical steps to address them.

Remember that the pain and setbacks are not signs of weakness, but are reminders that you are alive, striving, and courageous enough to chase after what truly matters to you. This commitment to your dreams and values, despite the odds, is the essence of fortitude. It is what makes life meaningful, and it is what will ultimately lead you to a deeper, more fulfilling existence.

So, what's next in this book?

In the next chapter, we delve into the core of your identity—your values and vision. This chapter is designed to help you understand what truly matters to you and how to align your actions with these fundamental principles. By clearly defining your values and creating a compelling vision for your future, you'll gain a stronger sense of purpose and direction. This foundation is crucial for developing fortitude and resilience in the face of life's challenges.

Moving forward, you'll explore the concept of approach vs. avoidance motivation. Understanding the difference between these two types of motivation can significantly impact your ability to achieve your goals. Approach motivation involves pursuing positive outcomes and striving toward desirable goals, while avoidance motivation focuses on evading negative outcomes. By shifting your focus to approach motivation, you can enhance your drive, reduce stress, and improve your overall well-being.

The following chapter delves into the psychological and neurological underpinnings of self-efficacy. Self-efficacy is the belief in your ability to succeed in specific situations or accomplish tasks. This chapter will provide insights into how self-efficacy is formed and maintained, and offer practical strategies to strengthen your confidence. By understanding the science behind self-efficacy, you'll be better equipped to tackle challenges and persevere through difficulties.

After that, we will explore the importance of facing the situations you tend to avoid. Avoidance can often lead to increased anxiety and missed opportunities for growth. This chapter will help you understand the benefits of confronting your fears and provide strategies for gradually exposing yourself to uncomfortable situations. By learning to face what you've been avoiding, you'll build resilience and fortitude.

Drawing on philosophical and psychological research, the next chapter will teach you how to prioritize eudaimonic well-being. Eudaimonia refers to a deep sense of fulfillment that comes from living a life aligned with your true self and values. This chapter will explore how to cultivate eudaimonic well-being through meaningful activities and relationships, rather than simply seeking pleasure or avoiding pain.

Moving ahead, the following chapter will help you understand and accept grief as a natural, meaningful part of the human experience. Grief can be incredibly challenging, but it's also an essential process for healing and growth. This chapter will provide insights into the stages of grief, the importance of acknowledging your feelings, and ways to find meaning and purpose through your loss.

Next, we will discover how exercise boosts mood, reduces anxiety, and improves cognitive function, providing a solid foundation for facing life's challenges. Physical activity is not only beneficial for your body but also has profound effects on your mental health. This chapter will explore the science behind these benefits and offer practical tips for incorporating exercise into your daily routine.

After that, you'll learn how producing exceptional work aligns with Stoic principles and contributes to personal and professional growth. The Stoic philosophy emphasizes discipline, focus, and resilience. This chapter will show you how to apply these principles to your work, enhancing your productivity and sense of accomplishment.

We'll then explore the balance between intense focus and calm perseverance. Finding the right balance between these two states is crucial for sustained success and well-being. This chapter will provide strategies for maintaining focus without burning out and for staying calm and persistent in the face of challenges.

Finally, you will learn to cherish the neutral moments in life. While we often focus on highs and lows, neutral moments also hold significant value. This chapter will teach you how to appreciate these moments, find contentment in the everyday, and cultivate a sense of peace and gratitude.

I hope that my learnings from life will serve you in your fight as well.

2. The Blueprint Within: Your Values & Vision

Imagine a tree, standing tall amidst storms. Just as a tree's roots anchor it firmly to the ground, enabling it to withstand storms and adverse weather, my values and vision have always grounded me, providing stability and resilience in the face of life's challenges. My values, which you can just think of as, my deeply held beliefs which are important to me, act as the core of my identity, much like roots are to a tree. Knowing what I stand for keeps me firm even when external circumstances are tumultuous. They have served as guiding principles that influence my decisions and actions. In moments of crisis, they act as a moral compass, helping me make choices that align with my true self. This alignment brings a sense of inner peace and confidence, much like how that tree stands tall and firm despite strong winds. When we hold onto our values, we draw strength from within, which empowers us to face difficulties with courage and resilience. Just as a tree draws nutrients and water through its roots to stay healthy and strong, our values nourish our spirit, helping us to thrive during those storms.

Vision is the clear and compelling picture of what we want our future to look like. It acts as a beacon, guiding our actions and decisions towards our desired destination. Like a tree growing towards the light, our vision directs our growth and progress, ensuring we are always moving forward, even when faced with obstacles. Having a vision has provided a sense of purpose and meaning in my life. It has given something to strive for and look forward to, which is crucial for maintaining motivation and hope.

A clear vision helps me stay focused and resilient, during the storms. When storms of life hit, our vision reminds us of what we are working towards, encouraging us to persevere. Just as a tree's roots help it to withstand storms by keeping it firmly planted, our vision helps us weather life's challenges by keeping us focused on our goals.

When our values and vision are aligned, they create a powerful foundation for resilience. Our values keep us grounded in who we are, while our vision guides us towards who we want to become. This alignment ensures that our actions are consistent with our beliefs and aspirations, providing a strong sense of coherence and purpose. Just as trees continuously grow and strengthen their roots, we must constantly nurture our values and vision. Regular self-reflection and adaptation help us stay true to our core beliefs while evolving towards our goals. This continuous growth reinforces our resilience, enabling us to withstand and grow from life's inevitable challenges. Our values and vision can also act as a support system. In times of adversity, revisiting our core values and vision can remind us of our strength and purpose, offering comfort and motivation. Like the roots of a tree intertwining and supporting each other, our values and vision can create a network of inner support that helps us stand firm and resilient.

On the flip side, and unfortunately as in with most people, when they don't know what they stand to represent or what their values are, it makes them breeze through life without a direction at all. And everything seems meaningless and hopeless to them. Especially, "fighting after loss".

You see, when you don't have a clear sense of what you choose to uphold as right or wrong your life will always attract all kinds of experiences your way. Most of the time, these experiences usually create a deteriorated picture of your reality. As simple as this problem sounds, not knowing your values is the singular reason why you make terrible life destructive decisions.

Most people really think the major cause of their problems is out there in the wild, vast ocean of this cosmic universal.

- They think if they weather wasn't gloomy; they'd be able to achieve their goals.
- Or if they came from a wealthy family, they'd have had a better life.
- Some even think the economy is the major reason why their lives is the way it is.

While all that might be true, but your life is a dance between what happens to you and what you make happen. And if you don't make yourself aware of what you really care about and strive to move in that direction, then you, yourself are not doing any better than your fate which apparently already seems to be working against you. You and I, might feel that our fate is working against us, but it only makes it more important for us to work in our favor. And how do you act in your favor? You act in accord with your values. I would feel orphaned if I had to abandon my values.

Though fate may seem against us, it becomes even more vital for us to act in our favor by staying true to our values. Abandoning them would leave us orphaned, but embracing them empowers us to put up a fight against our fate.

You often attribute your experiences to external forces, giving them more credit or blame than you give yourself. This tendency, known as an external locus of control, can lead to feelings of helplessness and diminished personal agency. However, living by your values is a choice, one that resides firmly within your control. Embracing an internal locus of control—where you recognize your power to influence your own life—can significantly enhance your sense of autonomy and well-being.

Psychological research shows that individuals with a strong internal locus of control are generally more proactive, resilient, and successful in achieving their goals. This decision to live by your values is a powerful assertion of your agency and will inevitably lead to both positive and negative consequences. While these consequences might fall beyond your control, you can take solace in knowing that your actions were in complete alignment with your identity and core beliefs.

Living in alignment with your values has been linked to greater life satisfaction and emotional well-being. According to self-determination theory, the fulfillment of basic psychological needs—autonomy, competence, and relatedness—is essential for psychological growth and well-being. When you act according to your values, you are fulfilling these needs, thereby enhancing your overall sense of happiness and fulfillment.

By making choices grounded in your values, you anchor yourself amid life's uncertainties. This congruence between your actions and your values creates a sense of coherence and purpose, which is crucial for mental health. When you face the outcomes, whether they are favorable or challenging, you will not feel completely lost, for you have stayed true to who you are. This alignment provides clarity and direction, guiding you through the consequences with a steadfast sense of self.

Now let's identify our greatest gift which will in turn help us in identifying our values and build our vision.

During my early days of finding meaning in life, I discovered this exercise and when I did it diligently, my findings changed my perspective.

Are you ready? Good!

As you're reading this, try to stand apart from yourself. Try to project your consciousness upward into a corner of the room and see yourself, in your mind's eye, reading.

Can you look at yourself almost as though you were someone else?

Now try something else. Think about the mood you're now in

Can you identify it? What are you feeling? How would you describe your present mental state?

Now think for a minute about how your mind is working. Is it quick and alert? Do you sense that you are torn between doing this mental exercise and evaluating the point to be made out of it?

If you really did that exercise, you'd have noticed something strange (or rather) fascinating about yourself. I learnt about this exercise when I read the **7 Habits of Highly Effective People by Stephen Covey**.

In that book Covey used this exercise to demonstrate that. *"Your ability to do what you just did is uniquely human. Animals do not possess this ability"*. He added that. *"We call this ability **'self-**

awareness *or the ability to think about your very thought process".*

He went on to assert that. *"We are not our feelings. We are not our moods. We are not even our thoughts. The very fact that we can think about these things separates us from them and from the animal world. Self-awareness enables us to stand apart and examine even the way we "see" ourselves".*

Self-Awareness, is the key to find your values and your vision.

Self-awareness is the conscious knowledge of one's own character, feelings, motives, and desires. It is a critical skill that allows individuals to gain a deeper understanding of themselves, which is essential for identifying and living by their core values. Here's how self-awareness can be helpful in knowing your values:

Self-awareness helps you recognize what genuinely motivates you and what you find meaningful. This understanding enables you to distinguish between what you value and what others may expect you to value. Through introspection, you can uncover the beliefs and principles that you hold dear. These beliefs form the foundation of your values. It allows you to reflect on past experiences and identify moments when you felt most fulfilled and authentic. These peak moments often highlight your core values. By honestly evaluating past mistakes and understanding the underlying reasons for your actions, you can gain insights into values that you may have compromised and which are important to uphold in the future. Being self-aware also helps you recognize and understand your emotional responses to different situations. Strong emotional reactions can signal when a core value is being honored or violated. Identifying patterns in your emotional responses can reveal consistent values that influence your behavior and decisions.

Now let's put Self-Awareness to use.

Exercise: Self-Awareness and Value Identification

Objective: This combined exercise will help you enhance self-awareness and discover your core values, providing a strong foundation for living a purposeful and authentic life.

Part 1: Self-Reflection and Emotional Awareness

Step 1: Reflect on Peak Experiences

1. **Think about your life's highlights:** Reflect on three to five peak experiences or moments when you felt truly happy, fulfilled, and at peace.

2. **Describe each experience:** Write a short description of each experience, including where you were, who you were with, what you were doing, and why it felt significant.

Step 2: Identify Common Themes

1. **Review your descriptions:** Look for common themes or patterns that emerge from your peak experiences.

2. **List the themes:** Write down the themes or qualities that stand out (e.g., adventure, connection, creativity, achievement).

Step 3: Track Emotional Responses

1. **Emotional Tracking:** For one week, keep a diary of your emotional responses to different situations. Note the situation, your feelings, and the intensity of those feelings.

2. **Pattern Recognition:** At the end of the week, review your diary and look for patterns or recurring themes in your emotional responses.

Part 2: Explore and Define Your Values

Step 4: Explore and Define Values

1. **Choose the top themes:** Select the top five to seven themes from your peak experiences and emotional tracking that resonate most deeply with you.

2. **Define each value:** For each chosen theme, write a brief definition of what it means to you. Consider why it is important and how it influences your actions and decisions.

Step 5: Prioritize Your Values

1. **Rank your values:** Rank your defined values in order of importance, from most to least significant. This helps clarify which values are non-negotiable and central to your identity.

2. **Reflect on your top values:** Consider how these values manifest in your daily life and how they guide your choices.

Part 3: Align Actions and Monitor Progress

Step 6: Align Your Actions with Your Values

1. **Assess alignment:** Reflect on how well your current actions, decisions, and lifestyle align with your identified values. Identify any discrepancies.

2. **Set goals for alignment:** Write down specific goals or actions you can take to better align your life with your core values. Be specific about what changes you need to make.

Step 7: Monitor and Adjust

1. **Regularly review your values:** Schedule regular check-ins (e.g., monthly or quarterly) to review your values and assess how well you are living in accordance with them.

2. **Adjust as needed:** Life circumstances and personal growth can lead to shifts in values. Be open to revisiting and adjusting your values as you evolve.

Give yourself plenty of time to determine your values. Start aligning your actions with your values. Get more comfortable in this new kind of lifestyle, and then come back to this page for one more exercise. Once you feel that you have reflected on how your values actualize in your life, it is time for starting again. And this time, we will start with the end in mind.

Exercise: The Story of Your Life

Exercise: Building Your Life Vision

Objective: This exercise will help you create a clear and compelling vision for your life, which serves as a roadmap to guide your decisions, actions, and goals.

Step 1: Envision Your Ideal Future

1. **Find a Quiet Space:**
   - Set aside uninterrupted time in a quiet space where you can reflect deeply.

2. **Visualization Exercise:**
   - Close your eyes and imagine your ideal future. Picture yourself 5, 10, or even 20 years from now.

- Consider all aspects of your life: personal, professional, relationships, health, hobbies, and contributions to the community.

3. **Describe Your Ideal Day:**
   - Write a detailed description of your ideal day in the future. Include:
     - Where you are living and what your surroundings look like.
     - What kind of work or activities you are engaged in.
     - Who you are spending time with.
     - How you are feeling emotionally and physically.
     - What values and principles guide your actions.

Step 2: Identify Key Themes and Goals

1. **Review Your Description:**
   - Read through your ideal day description and highlight key themes, activities, and feelings that stand out.

2. **Identify Core Elements:**
   - List the core elements that are essential to your vision. These might include:
     - Career aspirations and achievements.
     - Relationships and social connections.
     - Health and wellness goals.
     - Personal growth and development.
     - Hobbies and passions.

- Contributions to the community or causes.

3. **Set Long-Term Goals:**

   o Based on the core elements, write down specific long-term goals you want to achieve.

Step 3: Break Down Goals into Actionable Steps

1. **Prioritize Your Goals:**

   o Rank your long-term goals in order of importance to you.

2. **Create Action Plans:**

   o For each long-term goal, break it down into smaller, actionable steps.

   o Identify resources, skills, and support you will need to achieve each step.

3. **Set Milestones:**

   o Establish milestones and deadlines for each actionable step to track your progress.

Step 4: Align with Your Values

1. **Reflect on Your Values:**

   o Consider how each goal and action aligns with your core values. Make adjustments if necessary to ensure your vision is consistent with your values.

2. **Create a Values Statement:**

o Write a values statement that encapsulates your guiding principles. Refer to this statement when making decisions to ensure they align with your vision.

Step 5: Visualize Regularly and Adjust

1. Regular Visualization:

- Set aside time regularly (e.g. once in two months) to visualize your ideal future and reinforce your vision.

2. Review and Adjust:

- Periodically review your goals and action plans. Reflect on your progress and make adjustments as needed to stay aligned with your vision and values.

3. Celebrate Achievements:

- Acknowledge and celebrate your milestones and achievements along the way. This reinforces your commitment and motivation to your vision.

Before moving on to the next chapter, I want to tell you that yes these are just plans. Our fate might completely ruin it. But you need to remind yourself this:

Though fate may seem against us, it becomes even more vital for us to act in our favor by staying true to our values. Abandoning them would leave us orphaned, but embracing them empowers us to put up a fight against our fate.

3. Chase your Goals, Don't Get Chased by Anti-Goals!

In the previous chapter, you discovered how to define goals that truly resonate with your soul. A few years ago, I observed an intriguing phenomenon within myself, and through further research, I unearthed a profound insight. Allow me to guide you on this fascinating piece of information.

The pursuit of goals is a fundamental aspect of human motivation and well-being. However, the way we frame these pursuits can significantly impact our success and satisfaction.

Psychological research distinguishes between two types of motivation: approach and avoidance. Approach motivation involves moving towards a desired outcome or goal, driven by positive incentives such as personal growth, achievement, and fulfillment. In contrast, avoidance motivation involves moving away from undesirable outcomes or threats, driven by negative incentives such as fear, anxiety, and discomfort.

Studies have shown that approach motivation is associated with greater well-being, higher levels of satisfaction, and improved performance. Individuals who focus on what they want to achieve are more likely to experience positive emotions, sustain their efforts, and achieve their goals. On the other hand, avoidance motivation is linked to increased stress, anxiety, and burnout. When people concentrate on what they want to avoid, they are more likely to experience negative emotions, which can hinder their progress and overall well-being.

Research in cognitive psychology suggests that how we frame our goals can significantly influence our motivation and outcomes. Positive framing, which involves focusing on what we want to achieve, is more effective than negative framing, which involves focusing on what we want to avoid. Positive framing enhances our sense of agency and self-efficacy, leading to greater persistence and resilience.

For example, a study published in the "Journal of Personality and Social Psychology" found that individuals who set approach-oriented goals (e.g., "I want to improve my health by exercising regularly") were more likely to stick to their plans and achieve their objectives compared to those who set avoidance-oriented goals (e.g., "I want to avoid getting sick by not being sedentary").

Even one of the central tenets of Stoicism is the distinction between what is within our control and what is not. The Stoics believed that we should focus our efforts on what we can control—our thoughts, actions, and responses—while accepting what we cannot control. Applying this principle to goal setting, Stoicism encourages us to set goals based on our values and actions rather than external outcomes. By focusing on what we can actively pursue and influence, we align ourselves with approach motivation, which leads to greater internal satisfaction and tranquility. This aligns with the psychological concept of self-efficacy, where belief in our ability to influence outcomes fosters motivation and resilience.

If your mindset is all about just wanting to run away from your anti-goals without running towards your goals. Then, technically, you're still nowhere near your goals!

The Stoics also emphasized the importance of embracing challenges and adversities as opportunities for growth and development. This mindset encourages us to view obstacles not as threats to be avoided but as valuable experiences that contribute to our personal growth. By adopting an approach-oriented mindset, we transform potential setbacks into stepping stones towards our goals. Sometime ago, in the early 2000s, a psychologist named Carol Dweck carried out a research, which became the background work to the wonderful book she titled; *Mindset – changing the way you think to fulfill your potentials*.

Listen to her words carefully,

"when I was a young researcher, just starting out, something happened that changed my life. I was obsessed with understanding how people cope with failures, and I decided to study it by watching how students grapple with hard problems. So I brought children one at a time to a room in their school, made them comfortable, and then gave them a series of puzzles to solve".

It gets interesting here. Her findings gave the study of human psychology a shocking revelation. Keep reading;

"The first ones were fairly easy, but the next ones were hard. As the students grunted, perspired and toiled. I watched their strategies and probed what they were thinking and feeling. I expected differences among children in how they coped with the difficulty, but I saw something I never expected".

"Gasp! What could that be?"

"Confronted with the hard puzzles, one ten –year-old boy pulled up his chair, rubbed his hands together, smacked his lips, and cried out, 'I love a challenge!' Another, sweating away on these puzzles, looked up with a pleased expression and said with authority, 'You know, I was hoping this would be informative!'".

Well, her story didn't end there; let's see what happened afterwards in Dr. Carol Dweck's research.

"For thirty years, my research has shown that the view you adopt for yourself profoundly affects the way you lead your life. It can determine whether you become the person you want to be and whether you accomplish the things you value".

With her research findings, she went on to propose that there are two types of mindset, the fixed mindset and the growth mindset. The fixed mindset, Dweck explained, is a set of beliefs you hold that your qualities are carved in stone and this creates an urgency to prove yourself over and over.

This means, you believe you only have a certain amount of intelligence, a certain personality, and a certain moral character, therefore, you have one consuming goal of proving yourself over and over. You evaluate every situation with these questions; *Will I succeed or fail? Will I look smart or dumb? Will I be accepted or rejected? Will I feel like a winner or a loser?*

According to Dr. Carol Dweck, the moment you have the fixed mindset, you'd constantly want to prove yourself and whenever you're faced with a challenge, you give up at the slightest chance with a belief of being a failure.

With the fixed mindset in mind, if you solely focus on trying to avoid anti-goals, but fate strikes you with an experience, say a bad grade or death of a loved one, you'd feel like that experience serve as a yardstick to measure your capacity.

You Need Growth Mindset

"People are all born with a love of learning, but the fixed mindset can undo it." - Dr. Carol Dweck, as disturbing as that sounds, you and I can consider coming to a point of agreement that there's an atom of truth to that statement.

To support this disturbing fact, the only way you can truly move towards your goals is by developing ***"a mindset based on the belief in change"***, which Dweck called ***"Growth Mindset"***.

She added, ***"And the most gratifying part of my work is watching people change. Nothing is better than seeing people find their way to things they value"***.

In our context, finding your way to the things you value, means developing the love of learning and having a mindset based on the belief in change, so that you can chase your goals, without having to obsessing about anti-goals.

Now when we look at this idea of the "Growth Mindset" closely, you'd notice that, contrary to the fixed mindset, there's a love of learning and a belief in change.

But changing from the belief of running away from anti-goals – the fixed mindset – to running towards your goals – the growth mindset, requires a gradual process of reinforcing a particular belief system.

Dweck puts it this way, *"It means that change isn't like surgery. Even when you change, the old beliefs aren't just removed like a worn-out hip or knee and replaced with better ones".*

She added, *"Instead, the new belief take their place alongside the old ones, and as they become stronger, they give you a different way to think, feel, and act.*

Let me integrate these psychological and philosophical insights for you:

Setting Approach-Oriented Goals

To apply what we just learnt in our lives, we can start by setting approach-oriented goals that reflect our values and aspirations. Instead of framing goals in terms of what we want to avoid, we should articulate them in terms of what we want to achieve. For example, instead of saying, "I want to avoid failure in my career," we can say, "I want to excel and find fulfillment in my career."

Developing a Growth Mindset

The growth mindset, as proposed by psychologist Carol Dweck, complements the approach-oriented perspective by emphasizing the importance of learning and growth over fixed abilities. By believing that our abilities can be developed through effort and perseverance, we are more likely to embrace challenges and persist in the face of obstacles. This mindset encourages us to run towards our goals with confidence and determination.

Practicing Mindfulness and Self-Reflection

Regular mindfulness practice and self-reflection can help us stay aligned with our values and approach-oriented goals. By taking time to reflect on our motivations, we can ensure that our actions are guided by positive aspirations rather than fear and avoidance. Mindfulness also helps us stay present and focused, reducing the impact of stress and anxiety associated with avoidance motivation. This will help in reinforcing the new belief system.

4. Believe that you have what it Takes

Whether you find yourself in a battle where your life is facing serious challenges from your fate, or you find yourself being blessed with truly valuable things in life, you have a similar situation at hand. In the former one, every moment becomes pivotal, you need to think on your feet, take decisions and make things happen to fight back and protect what means the world to you. But you might not feel confident enough to make those decisions and act swiftly. In the latter one, you might feel like you don't truly deserve those blessings. You feel like an imposter and you don't truly enjoy the bliss. You don't believe in yourself.

I had serious doubts about myself, my abilities, and potentials earlier in my life. Feeling like an imposter, thoughts of doubt, disbelief, fear of failure, and fear of rejection made my mind a chaotic place. And so is the case with most people. In fact, we as a society don't put the due importance on having a peaceful mind. We normalize chaos, the merit of which, I can understand but at least aiming for a peaceful mind should also be cherished. It requires work, and if we as a society could appreciate the ones who put in those efforts, we would be living in a much better world. Mihaly Csikszentmihalyi, the most prominent psychologist in my knowledge, had something similar to say:

"At certain times in history cultures have taken it for granted that a person wasn't fully human unless he or she learned to master thoughts and feeling. In

Confucian China, in ancient Sparta, in Republican Rome, in the early Pilgrim settlements of New England, and among the British upper classes of the Victorian era, people were held responsible for keeping a tight rein on their emotions. Anyone who indulged in self-pity, who let instinct rather than reflection dictate actions, forfeited the right to be accepted as a member of the community. In other historical periods, such as the one in which we are now living, the ability to control oneself is not held in high esteem. But, it seems that those who take the trouble to gain mastery over what happens in consciousness do live a happier life".

He wrote further:

"To achieve such mastery it is obviously important to understand how consciousness works. The function of consciousness is to represent information about what is happening outside and inside the organism in such a way that it can be evaluated and acted upon by the body. In this sense, it functions as a clearing house for sensations, perceptions, feelings and ideas, establishing priorities among all the diverse information. Without consciousness, we would still "know" what is going on, but we would have to react to it in a reflexive, instinctive way. With consciousness, we can deliberately weigh what the senses tell us, and respond accordingly. A person can make himself happy, or miserable, regardless of what is actually happening 'outside,' just by changing the contents of consciousness".

In simple terms, the chaos of our mind is majorly the consequence of our own negligence. Our mind can become our enemy on its own, but to turn it into a friend, efforts are required. And fortunately belief in one's abilities has a tangible impact on brain function. Neuroplasticity, the brain's ability to reorganize itself by forming new neural connections, shows that our thoughts and beliefs can literally shape our brain. Positive affirmations and visualizations can enhance this process, reinforcing our belief in our abilities. Research in neuroplasticity reveals that regularly engaging in positive self-talk and visualization can strengthen neural pathways associated with confidence and resilience. For instance, athletes who visualize their performance and success can improve their actual performance by creating and reinforcing the neural networks involved in those actions.

Your fortitude is closely tied to the concept of self-efficacy. Coined by psychologist Albert Bandura, self-efficacy is the belief in one's ability to succeed in specific situations. This belief significantly influences how people approach goals, challenges, and setbacks. Self-efficacy is defined as the belief in one's capabilities to organize and execute the courses of action required to manage prospective situations. It differs from self-esteem, which is a general feeling of self-worth, in that self-efficacy is task-specific. A person might have high self-efficacy in academic settings but low self-efficacy in social situations.

One of the key components of Self-Efficacy are **Mastery Experiences**. Mastery experiences are the successes in the past that build a robust belief in one's abilities. These experiences are the most effective way to build self-efficacy. This is the why with every time your fate hits you and you fall but fight your way back to standing up again, you gain more fortitude. You become more powerful. This experience of standing up when you were knocked down has not just saved you at this particular moment, but it has contributed to the reservoir of energy that you can tap into, the next time your fate will hit you. This is like a super power. Every time you are broken and you fight to redeem yourself, you become stronger than ever.

The second component is **Social Modeling**. Observing others successfully completing a task can strengthen the observer's belief in their own abilities. There is no better man on earth than David Goggins to look up to, if you want to use this component to build your fortitude. I have listened to David Goggins while working out for hours. And the only reason he speaks is to help people like you and me to utilize this component to cultivate belief in ourself. If he can do it, we can. Go and look him up on the internet if you don't know him yet.

The third component is **Social Persuasion** (I also consider **Self-Persuasion** as equally effective if done right). Encouragement from others can help an individual overcome self-doubt and focus on their effort and perseverance. Not all of us are lucky enough to have someone who can encourage us. But if you have someone who genuinely wants to see you grow, who talks positively about your abilities and believes in you, go talk to them. And if you don't have someone like that in your life, it is still fine. Go stand in front of a mirror and tell yourself that you got what it takes. I have done it countless times in my life. I back it with actually showing up for the things I know I should be doing. When you say things to yourself and then you back them up with actions (by just showing up to make efforts), you will take your own encouragement seriously.

Self-efficacy contributes to fortitude in several ways. Individuals with high self-efficacy are better equipped to handle stress. You will perceive challenging situations as manageable and will be less likely to be overwhelmed by them. This will allow you to bounce back from setbacks more effectively. People with strong self-efficacy are more likely to persist in the face of adversity. You will view obstacles as challenges to be overcome rather than insurmountable barriers. Your persistence is a core component of your fortitude. Self-efficacious individuals approach problems with a solution-oriented mindset. You will be more likely to engage in proactive problem-solving and find innovative ways to overcome difficulties. Remember? "when everybody zigs, you zag". It is also associated with positive emotions such as optimism and enthusiasm. These emotions provide the energy and motivation needed to confront challenges and sustain effort over time. When you believe in your abilities, you are less afraid of failure. This reduced fear allows you to take risks and pursue your goals with confidence, contributing to your overall resilience and fortitude.

Here are practical strategies to develop and strengthen self-efficacy:

1. Set Achievable Goals

Start with small, attainable goals that build your confidence. Success in these goals can create a positive feedback loop that reinforces your belief in your abilities.

Example: If you aim to improve your fitness, start with a manageable exercise routine. Gradually increase the intensity and duration as you achieve each milestone.

2. Reflect on Past Successes

Regularly reflecting on your previous successes and the strengths you utilized to accomplish them can reinforce your self-efficacy.

Example: Keep a journal of your achievements. Write down what you did, how you did it, and the skills you used. Reviewing this journal can remind you of your capabilities during challenging times.

3. Practice Positive Self-Talk

Replace negative thoughts with positive affirmations. This practice can help you maintain a positive mindset and reinforce your self-belief.

Example: Instead of thinking, "I can't do this," tell yourself, "I have the skills and determination to overcome this challenge."

4. Seek Social Support

Engage with people and environments that uplift and support you. Positive social interactions can reinforce your belief in your capabilities.

Example: Surround yourself with friends, family, or colleagues who encourage you and believe in your abilities. Their support can boost your confidence.

5. Observe Role Models

Identify role models who have achieved what you aspire to accomplish. Their journeys can provide a roadmap for your own success. (major hint: DAVID GOGGINS)

Example: Follow individuals in your field who have demonstrated resilience and success. Learn from their strategies and mindset.

6. Manage Stress Effectively

Learning to manage stress and anxiety can prevent these feelings from undermining your belief in your abilities.

Example: Practice stress-reduction techniques such as mindfulness, meditation, and deep-breathing exercises. These practices can help you stay calm and focused.

7. Embrace Challenges

View challenges as opportunities to learn and grow rather than as threats to your competence. This mindset shift can enhance your resilience and fortitude.

Example: When faced with a difficult task, remind yourself that it is a chance to develop new skills and demonstrate your capabilities.

5. Adapt to Whatever you are Escaping From

One summer, in a small village nestled at the base of a towering mountain, lived a young girl named Aisha. Aisha was known for her laughter, bright eyes, and boundless curiosity. However, one fear overshadowed her vibrant spirit—the fear of the dark forest that surrounded their village. Tales of wild animals, treacherous paths, and eerie noises kept Aisha from venturing beyond the village's borders.

One day, a fierce storm hit the village. Torrential rains and howling winds wreaked havoc, and Aisha's beloved goat, Nala, went missing. The villagers searched high and low but found no trace of Nala. As dusk approached, Aisha realized that Nala had likely wandered into the dark forest.

Despite her fear, Aisha knew she had to find Nala. With a heart pounding in her chest, she took a deep breath, grabbed a lantern, and stepped into the forest. The familiar stories of danger echoed in her mind with every step, but the thought of Nala alone and frightened in the storm pushed her forward.

As she ventured deeper into the forest, Aisha found that the tales she had heard were only half true. Yes, there were shadows and strange sounds, but there was also beauty—a glimmer of fireflies, the scent of pine, and the rustling of leaves in the wind. Slowly, her fear began to fade, replaced by a sense of determination and discovery.

After hours of searching, Aisha found Nala tangled in a thicket. Relief and triumph surged through her as she carefully freed her goat. As they made their way back to the village, Aisha realized that the forest was no longer a place of fear. By facing it head-on, she had uncovered a strength and courage she didn't know she possessed.

Sometimes what is dear to us and we are lacking in our lives, is hidden in a scary dark forest which we tend to avoid. For some, this could be a better relationship with their parents or an audience who would really get inspired with our art. But we escape the possibility of conflicts due to difference in opinion with our parents or we avoid the possibility of being judged by people for not being perfect at what we are creating. What we truly value lies beyond the things we are trying to escape from. But the unfortunate fact is that we don't even realize what are we escaping from.

When faced with stress and anxiety, our natural reaction is often to flee or avoid the source of discomfort. From a psychological perspective, anxiety and fear are powerful motivators of avoidance behavior. The amygdala, a part of the brain involved in emotional processing, triggers a fight-or-flight response when faced with perceived threats. This response can lead to the avoidance of situations that are actually crucial for personal growth. Over time, this habitual avoidance becomes automatic, making individuals unaware that they are escaping from situations that hold significant value for them.

We don't even make fresh attempts at making these situations better. Martin Seligman's theory of learned helplessness explains that when individuals repeatedly encounter situations where they feel they have no control, they may develop a mindset of helplessness. This mindset can lead to the avoidance of new challenges, as the individual believes they are incapable of overcoming them. This unconscious avoidance of potential growth opportunities stems from past experiences of perceived failure.

This avoidance behavior provides temporary relief but can lead to increased anxiety, missed opportunities, and reduced psychological resilience in the long term. Cognitive Behavioral Therapy (CBT) identifies avoidance as a maladaptive coping strategy that reinforces anxiety. Understanding avoidance behavior is the first step in learning how to adapt to what you are escaping from. Recognizing when you are avoiding a situation can help you address it directly.

The Role of Acceptance

Acceptance is a foundational principle in many psychological therapies, including Acceptance and Commitment Therapy (ACT). It involves embracing your thoughts, feelings, and experiences without judgment and understanding that these experiences are part of the human condition. ACT encourages individuals to accept their experiences and commit to actions that align with their values. Research has shown that ACT can reduce symptoms of anxiety and depression and improve overall psychological flexibility. Accepting what you are escaping from allows you to face it without the added burden of judgment or resistance. This acceptance is a crucial step toward adaptation.

Building Psychological Flexibility

Psychological flexibility is the ability to adapt to changing circumstances, shift perspectives, and balance competing desires and needs. It is a key component of resilience and fortitude. Research has shown that individuals with high psychological flexibility are better able to cope with stress, adapt to change, and maintain well-being in the face of adversity. This flexibility involves changing behaviors to meet the demands of different situations, which is associated with better problem-solving skills and more effective coping strategies. Developing psychological flexibility helps you adapt to new and challenging situations, reducing the need to escape and increasing your capacity to thrive.

Reframing Challenges

Reframing is a cognitive-behavioral technique that involves changing the way you perceive a situation. By viewing challenges as opportunities for growth rather than threats, you can reduce avoidance behaviors and increase your ability to adapt. Research in cognitive psychology suggests that reframing can reduce negative emotions and increase problem-solving abilities. Carol Dweck's research on growth mindset shows that individuals who believe their abilities can be developed through effort are more likely to embrace challenges and persist in the face of setbacks. Reframing challenges as opportunities for growth can reduce the desire to escape and increase your willingness to adapt and engage with difficult situations.

Developing Coping Strategies

When facing the inevitable challenges and stressors of life, effective coping strategies are crucial for adapting to what you are attempting to escape from. These strategies not only help manage stress and reduce anxiety but also build resilience and foster a sense of control over one's circumstances. By developing a diverse set of coping mechanisms, you can navigate through difficulties more effectively, transforming what was once a source of distress into an opportunity for growth and fortitude.

Problem-Focused Coping: Tackling Stress Head-On

Problem-focused coping involves directly addressing the source of stress by finding practical solutions to the problems at hand. This proactive approach can significantly lower stress levels and enhance psychological well-being. For instance, if financial troubles are a source of stress, problem-focused coping might involve creating a detailed budget, seeking additional income sources, or consulting a financial advisor. Research has consistently shown that individuals who employ problem-focused coping strategies experience lower levels of stress and higher levels of well-being compared to those who do not. By confronting the issue head-on, you reduce the urge to escape and increase your ability to adapt to the situation.

Emotion-Focused Coping: Managing the Emotional Fallout

While problem-focused coping addresses the external problem, emotion-focused coping deals with the internal emotional responses to stress. Techniques such as mindfulness, relaxation exercises, and emotional expression are essential tools in this approach. Mindfulness, for example, helps you stay present and reduces the overwhelming impact of stress by encouraging a non-judgmental awareness of your thoughts and feelings. Relaxation exercises, such as deep breathing and progressive muscle relaxation, can help alleviate physical tension and promote a sense of calm. Emotional expression, whether through talking with a friend, journaling, or engaging in creative activities, allows you to process and release pent-up emotions. These techniques are invaluable for reducing the emotional burden of stress, thereby enhancing your overall well-being.

Building a Repertoire of Coping Strategies

Developing a repertoire of coping strategies is akin to building a personal toolkit for handling stress. This toolkit should include both problem-focused and emotion-focused strategies, allowing you to choose the most appropriate approach for any given situation. For example, while problem-focused coping might be ideal for addressing work-related stress, emotion-focused coping could be more effective for dealing with the grief of losing a loved one. The key is to have a flexible and adaptive mindset, ready to employ different strategies as circumstances change.

Reducing the Need to Escape

By effectively managing stress through a combination of problem-focused and emotion-focused coping strategies, you reduce the compulsion to escape from your problems. Instead of viewing challenges as insurmountable obstacles, you begin to see them as opportunities for growth and self-improvement. This shift in perspective is fundamental to building fortitude, as it fosters a proactive rather than reactive approach to life's difficulties.

Increasing Your Ability to Adapt

Adaptability is a hallmark of fortitude. When you develop effective coping strategies, you enhance your ability to adapt to changing circumstances. This adaptability is not about avoiding challenges but rather about facing them with resilience and resourcefulness. Whether it's navigating a career change, coping with a health diagnosis, or handling interpersonal conflicts, the ability to adapt allows you to remain grounded and resilient in the face of adversity.

Integrating Coping Strategies into Daily Life

To fully benefit from effective coping strategies, it's essential to integrate them into your daily routine. Regular practice of mindfulness, consistent use of problem-solving techniques, and habitual emotional expression can make these strategies second nature. By embedding these practices into your daily life, you create a strong foundation for ongoing resilience and fortitude.

Now let us take one of the scenarios I was talking about in the beginning of this chapter to help you understand how to apply this.

Scenario:

You are trying to establish a better relationship with your parent, but your thought processes do not align, and talking with them gives you anxiety.

Applying Problem-Focused Coping

1. **Identify Specific Issues:**
   o Write down specific issues that cause conflict or anxiety when interacting with your parent. For example, it might be disagreements over lifestyle choices or political beliefs.

2. **Develop Solutions:**
   o Once the issues are identified, brainstorm potential solutions or compromises. For instance, if political discussions always lead to arguments, agree to avoid that topic during your conversations.

- Another solution might be setting boundaries. For example, you could agree to have shorter, more frequent conversations rather than long, potentially contentious ones.

3. **Seek Mediation or Counseling:**

    - Sometimes, a neutral third party, such as a family counselor or your elder sibling/cousin who already has a better relationship with them, can help facilitate discussions and offer strategies for better communication.

    - Mediation can provide a structured environment where both parties feel heard and understood, reducing the potential for anxiety-inducing conflicts.

Applying Emotion-Focused Coping

1. **Practice Mindfulness:**

    - Before and after interactions with your parent, practice mindfulness techniques to help manage anxiety. This could include deep breathing exercises, meditation, or progressive muscle relaxation.

    - Mindfulness can help you stay present and reduce the emotional impact of stress during the conversation.

2. **Use Relaxation Techniques:**

    - Engage in activities that promote relaxation and reduce stress, such as yoga, listening to calming music, or taking a walk.

    - These activities can help you manage the anxiety associated with interactions with your parent.

3. **Emotional Expression:**
   - Find healthy ways to express your emotions. This could be through journaling, talking to a supportive friend, or engaging in creative activities like painting or writing.
   - Expressing your feelings can help you process and release pent-up emotions, reducing the overall emotional burden.

Building a Repertoire of Coping Strategies

1. **Combine Approaches:**
   - Use a combination of problem-focused and emotion-focused strategies. For example, establish clear boundaries (problem-focused) while also practicing mindfulness before and after interactions (emotion-focused).

2. **Flexibility:**
   - Be flexible in your approach. If one strategy doesn't work, try another. For instance, if avoiding certain topics is not reducing anxiety, you might explore deeper emotional expression or seek professional advice.

Reducing the Need to Escape

1. **Shift Perspective:**
   - Instead of seeing the relationship as a source of stress, view it as an opportunity to practice and strengthen your coping strategies.
   - Recognize the efforts and progress made, no matter how small, to build a positive outlook towards the relationship.

2. **Positive Reinforcement:**

o   Reward yourself for successful interactions, no matter how minor they may seem. This can create positive reinforcement and reduce the desire to avoid the relationship.

Increasing Your Ability to Adapt

1. **Gradual Exposure:**

   o   Gradually increase the time and depth of your interactions with your parent. Start with short, positive conversations and slowly build up to longer, more meaningful discussions as your anxiety decreases.

2. **Self-Reflection:**

   o   Regularly reflect on your interactions and coping strategies. Consider what worked, what didn't, and how you can adapt your approach for future interactions.

3. **Ongoing Practice:**

   o   Make coping strategies a regular part of your routine, not just something you use during stressful interactions. Consistent practice will strengthen your resilience and adaptability.

Integrating Coping Strategies into Daily Life

1. **Routine Practice:**

   o   Integrate mindfulness and relaxation exercises into your daily routine. This can create a baseline of calm and readiness for any stressful situation.

2. **Ongoing Communication:**
   o Maintain regular, open lines of communication with your parent. Even if the conversations are brief, consistent contact can help build familiarity and reduce anxiety over time.

3. **Support Systems:**
   o Lean on friends, or family who can offer advice, empathy, and encouragement. Sharing your experiences with others can provide new perspectives and coping ideas.
   o Adapting to what you are escaping from involves developing and utilizing effective coping strategies. This proactive and adaptive mindset is key to building fortitude and thriving in the face of adversity.

6. Seek Joy, Not Pleasure

I remember the first time I came across the term "Eudaimonia". In my pursuit to understand life, and in an attempt to develop a suitable conceptual framework for my blog "Awesome Life Geek", I searched on google: "What can we call the concept of living in accordance with one's true values", the value of "Authenticity" popped up. On further research about authenticity as a way of life, I was finally introduced with the term "Eudaimonia" and it's opposite "Hedonism" as well. These concepts are the foundations of how I take decisions on a daily basis in my life and my habits are governed by the same.

Eudaimonia is often translated as "human flourishing". Rooted in ancient Greek philosophy, particularly the works of Aristotle, eudaimonic happiness focuses on living in accordance with one's true self and realizing one's full potential. Unlike hedonic happiness, which is about maximizing pleasure and minimizing pain, eudaimonic happiness involves living virtuously, fulfilling one's purpose, and achieving personal excellence.

Aristotle believed that true happiness comes from actualizing one's potential and living a life of virtue. This idea has been echoed throughout history and remains relevant in contemporary discussions about well-being and life satisfaction. **It feels utterly pompous to say this but I will still say it, "I agree with Aristotle!"**.

But I am not alone, psychological research, also suggests that true well-being and fortitude are more closely associated with seeking joy, which encompasses a deeper, more enduring sense of contentment. Pleasure is typically characterized by short-term gratification that stimulates the brain's reward centers. Activities that provide pleasure include eating delicious food, buying new clothes, or receiving praise. While these experiences can boost mood temporarily, they are not sustainable sources of happiness. The concept of the "hedonic treadmill" illustrates how people tend to return to a stable level of happiness despite significant positive or negative events. This phenomenon explains why the joy from pleasurable activities quickly fades, prompting a continuous cycle of seeking more pleasure to maintain the same level of happiness.

Joy, on the other hand, is a profound sense of well-being that arises from meaningful experiences, relationships, and achievements. Unlike pleasure, joy is not dependent on external stimuli and is often associated with personal growth, purpose, and connection. Modern psychological research distinguishes between eudaimonic and hedonic well-being. While hedonia focuses on pleasure, enjoyment, and the avoidance of discomfort, eudaimonia emphasizes meaning, personal growth, and self-realization.

Studies have shown that eudaimonic activities, such as volunteering, pursuing personal goals, and developing meaningful relationships, contribute more significantly to long-term well-being than purely hedonic activities. For example, a study by Ryff and Singer (2008) found that individuals who engage in eudaimonic activities report higher levels of life satisfaction and psychological well-being.

Seeking Joy and Not Pleasure does not mean that you have to make sure you are not having any kind of pleasure in your life. If you do so, you are being chased by an anti-goal. The better advice and title of this chapter would be prioritizing joy over pleasure. Seek joy, and let pleasure come into your life on its own, do not sweat over it.

The experiences of pleasure and joy, while both associated with positive emotions, engage different brain mechanisms. Understanding these distinctions can illuminate why pleasure is often short-lived, while joy leads to lasting fulfillment. And this will also help you understand the interplay between joy and pleasure.

Pleasure and the Brain's Reward Circuitry

Pleasure is primarily linked to the brain's reward circuitry, which includes structures like the nucleus accumbens, the ventral tegmental area (VTA), and the release of the neurotransmitter dopamine. These components form a pathway that reinforces behaviors by providing a sensation of pleasure and satisfaction.

Dopamine and Craving

Dopamine plays a crucial role in this process. When we engage in activities that we find pleasurable—such as eating delicious food, receiving praise, or buying something new—dopamine is released. This neurotransmitter is often referred to as the "feel-good" chemical because it creates feelings of euphoria and satisfaction.

However, dopamine is also associated with craving and the anticipation of reward. This means that while dopamine release can make us feel good in the moment, it also drives us to seek out these pleasurable experiences repeatedly. This cycle can lead to what we already talked about "the hedonic treadmill," where individuals continuously pursue short-term pleasures without achieving lasting satisfaction.

Joy and Broader Neural Networks

In contrast to the dopamine-driven pleasure pathways, the experience of joy engages broader neural networks that are associated with meaning, social bonding, and long-term well-being.

Prefrontal Cortex and Meaning

The prefrontal cortex, a region at the front of the brain, is heavily involved in the experience of joy. This area is responsible for higher-order functions such as planning, decision-making, and reflecting on life's meaning and purpose. When we engage in activities that align with our values and contribute to our sense of purpose, the prefrontal cortex is activated. This activation supports a deeper, more enduring sense of fulfillment compared to the transient pleasure provided by dopamine.

Oxytocin and Social Bonding

Another critical component in the experience of joy is the hormone oxytocin. Often referred to as the "love hormone," oxytocin is released during social interactions, such as hugging, bonding with loved ones, and acts of kindness. This hormone promotes feelings of trust, empathy, and connectedness, which are essential for building and maintaining meaningful relationships.

Oxytocin's role in social bonding helps explain why activities that foster connection and altruism contribute to a sustained sense of joy. Unlike the short-term pleasure associated with dopamine, the joy derived from social bonds and meaningful interactions is more stable and long-lasting.

The Interplay Between Pleasure and Joy

While pleasure and joy activate different brain mechanisms, they are not mutually exclusive. Engaging in pleasurable activities can contribute to overall well-being when balanced with pursuits that promote joy. For instance, enjoying a good meal (pleasure) with close friends (joy) can create a rich and fulfilling experience. However, prioritizing joy over pleasure is crucial for long-term happiness. By focusing on activities that engage the prefrontal cortex and oxytocin pathways—such as pursuing meaningful goals, building relationships, and contributing to the greater good—we can cultivate a deeper, more resilient form of happiness.

Social media is the greatest promoter of hedonic behaviors, providing instant gratification through quick laughs and confirmation on whatever we are thinking through relatable content, likes, comments, and shares. This leads to continuous supply of short-term pleasure but at the grand expense of deeper, more meaningful activities that contribute to eudaimonic happiness. Studies have shown that excessive social media use can lead to increased feelings of anxiety, depression, and loneliness. The constant comparison to others' highlight reels can further undermine our self-esteem and detract from our sense of fulfillment.

In the presence of such a vicious habit, you will need to be proactive in prioritizing joy over pleasure:

1. **Pursue your Vision and live in accordance with your Values:** The chapter on blueprint within, is your key here as well. Pursuing long-term goals that align with your core values is the path to joy. If for some reason, you have not completed the exercises of that chapter, make sure you do them because

without acting on those, nothing in this book can propel you forward.

2. **Cultivate Deep Relationships:** You will find another chapter on the same in this book because this is also one of the most essential way to experience joy in life. Invest time and energy in building and nurturing meaningful relationships. Focus on quality over quantity. Schedule regular catch-ups with close friends or family members. Plan activities that encourage deeper conversations.

3. **Engage in Altruistic Activities:** Participate in activities that benefit others and provide a sense of purpose. This can be as simple as helping your own friends selflessly at times, and as grandiose as taking social initiatives and standing actively for the causes you believe in. Altruism paves way for joy and greater good, not just for you but for other beings as well.

4. **Engage in Creative Activities:** For me, just drawing a simple sketch or writing a few lines of poetry give me so much joy that hours of social media scrolling can never give. Find ways to express yourself creatively, you are bound to find joy in that process. And do not engage in creative activities for merely showing it off to others, try to truly express your inner self. The quality of the art is not important here, the intent and expression is all you require to experience joy.

5. **Set Clear Boundaries with Social Media:** Use app timers or built-in screen time trackers to limit your daily social media use. Think of it as a parasite that eats your valuable free time which could otherwise be used to feed your own soul with joy. There is place for passive entertainment, I agree, but

on the cost of never being able to actively pursue joy? I think that cost is too hefty to bear. Set a daily limit of 30-45 minutes for social media use and stick to it. Be intentional about how and why you use social media. Before opening a social media app, ask yourself why you are doing so. Is it to connect with someone, seek information, or simply out of habit? Being mindful of your intentions can help you use social media more purposefully and less compulsively. Use your free time to first engage in activities that bring joy, such as reading, exercising, or spending quality time with loved ones and only then use the remaining time to interact with social media. This prioritization has helped me to curb my own compulsive habit.

6. **Stay away from consuming alcohol or smoking:** If this sounds controversial, so be it, this is my book, I have always dreamt of really helping out people going through the repeated setbacks in life. So I will not hold back my thoughts. I believe that one should not consume alcohol or smoke because not only it deteriorates health but it also diminishes the hunger to go after the things that will truly bring joy in your life. They serve as a shortcut, but a fake one. You can easily find pleasure in it, but you will never truly put as much efforts as you would otherwise, in pursuing joy in your life.

7. Accept Grief as the Final Stage of Love

My heart sinks while writing this chapter, so I understand how heavy it can be for you, who is reading it. But if there is anything in this world, I am most certain about, is this idea. I will not say that I have learnt it, I am yet to completely wrap my head around this truth, but my reluctance to fully accept it does not change it. I continue to accept it a bit more with each passing day. It is like sipping a little bit of poison every day. But it is necessary. It gives me the power to love from my bare soul, we will talk about that too in one of the following chapters.

Grief is the love we hold within us that we were unable to share with our departed beloved.

This is not the standard definition of grief, but this is the one which my heart has accepted and resonated with the most. We will talk about the stages of grief itself in this chapter, but the actual wisdom which I wanted to share with you here is just that ***all love transforms into grief one day***. This might be disheartening for you, but for some people, such as myself, this is liberating as well.

We obsess on the permanence of the relation which we share with the people we deeply love. We obsess over it so much that we often take those relations and the limited time we have with each other, for granted. A lot of meaningless, glittery things take the main stage and we care so much about the trivial things that we completely forget that the golden bond which we share with them is temporary. We are not grateful, present, involved, and selfless to cherish that bond.

If you must take one idea from this chapter, then it is that we need to normalize the grief that lies in our path of love. We need to accept it. From my own experience, to how much ever extent I have accepted this, I want to tell you that the dynamics of how you interact with your loved ones change forever. And it also serves you when life explicitly makes you aware of your own or your loved one's mortality. At that time, you don't stand and ask "Why Us?". You know that it is the destination for all the beautiful love that exists on this earth.

Your love has to transcend one day and your love just becomes as vast as this universe, and how lucky are you, that you will then never be able to outgrow it. You will always stay in its warmth.

That is all, I wanted to write about this.

Let's now understand the stages of the final stage of love itself: Grief.

Grief is an experience that affects us emotionally, physically, and psychologically. It encompasses a range of feelings, from sadness and anger to confusion and guilt. Understanding the nature of grief can help us accept it as a necessary and meaningful part of the human experience.

Elisabeth Kübler-Ross, a pioneering psychiatrist, introduced the concept of the five stages of grief in her 1969 book "On Death and Dying." These stages—denial, anger, bargaining, depression, and acceptance—offer a framework for understanding the complex emotional journey that individuals go through when dealing with significant loss.

Denial is often the first stage, where individuals struggle to accept the reality of the loss. This stage acts as a defense mechanism, numbing the immediate shock and allowing the person to slowly process the overwhelming emotions. It might involve disbelief and a sense of numbness or detachment.

Anger follows as the individual begins to confront the reality of the loss. This stage is characterized by feelings of frustration, helplessness, and sometimes directed anger towards others, the situation, or even the deceased. It serves as an emotional outlet, providing a temporary sense of structure to the chaos of grief.

Bargaining is the stage where the individual dwells on "what if" or "if only" statements, reflecting on ways they believe the situation could have been avoided. This stage involves an attempt to regain control through a negotiation with a higher power or through making promises and considering hypothetical scenarios.

Depression sets in when the individual fully acknowledges the loss and its implications. This stage is marked by deep sadness, withdrawal from life, and an overwhelming sense of emptiness. It is a crucial part of the grieving process, where the person confronts their sorrow and begins to process the loss more deeply.

Acceptance, the final stage, is where the individual comes to terms with the reality of the loss. It does not mean that the person is "okay" with what happened, but rather that they have found a way to live with it. In this stage, the individual integrates the loss into their life, finding a new way forward while still honoring the memory of their loved one. Acceptance brings a sense of peace and the ability to begin adjusting to life without the deceased.

While these stages provide a valuable framework, it is important to note that not everyone experiences them in a linear fashion. Some may skip stages, revisit certain stages multiple times, or experience them in a different order. Grief is a highly individual process, influenced by various factors such as the nature of the loss, personal resilience, and support systems. The stages of grief help normalize the emotions felt during bereavement, offering reassurance that the intense and often confusing feelings are a natural part of the healing journey.

Viktor Frankl, a renowned psychiatrist and Holocaust survivor, emphasized the importance of finding meaning in suffering. *"The true meaning of life is to be discovered in the world rather than within man or his own psyche, as if it were a closed system."*

As Alex Pattakos, co-author of Prisoners of Our Thoughts, expressed, *"We don't create meaning – we find it. "* He paused and continued. *"And we can't find it if we don't look for it. Sometimes it looms large in our lives; sometimes it slips in almost unobserved. Unfortunately, not everyone takes the time or makes the effort to find meaning in life's moments."*

"Taking time to reflect on the meaning of each of life's moments is the first step to opening ourselves to the deeper overall meaning of our individual lives.

By finding meaning in our loss, we can transform our grief into a source of growth and resilience. This does not diminish the pain but provides a pathway to healing and understanding.

I am sharing with you, in the title of this chapter, a meaning for loss. The meaning which I discovered myself and it has helped me through my pain and I deeply wish it can serve you as well.

8. Build Physical Strength as Well

Building fortitude includes not only emotional and mental resilience but also physical strength. But the most vital part about this is that when life throws overwhelming challenges our way, leaving us feeling lost and unsure of where to begin rebuilding. In such times of confusion and despair, focusing on physical strength and working out can serve as a **crucial starting point**. When life lacks structure due to unforeseen events—a sudden loss, a health diagnosis, a breakup—our mental and emotional states are thrown into disarray. In these moments, physical exercise offers several benefits that can help us regain a sense of control and direction. Exercise provides not only a structured routine but also tangible progress that can lay the groundwork for developing fortitude in other areas of life.

When everything feels out of control, establishing a regular workout routine can bring a sense of order to your life. Exercise requires planning and commitment, which can help you create a structured daily schedule. This newfound routine provides a foundation on which to build other positive habits. Physical activity increases blood flow to the brain, which can help clear mental fog and improve cognitive function. When you're overwhelmed, exercising can provide a mental break, allowing you to return to your problems with a clearer mind and renewed focus.

Research has shown that regular physical activity and strength training have profound effects on mental health. Engaging in physical exercise can improve mood, reduce anxiety and depression, and enhance cognitive function. These benefits are due to a combination of biological, psychological, and social factors.

Biological Mechanisms

Physical exercise triggers the release of endorphins, often referred to as "feel-good" hormones, which help reduce pain and improve mood. Additionally, exercise increases the production of brain-derived neurotrophic factor (BDNF), a protein that supports the growth and maintenance of neurons, enhancing brain health and cognitive function.

Psychological Mechanisms

Exercise provides a sense of accomplishment and self-efficacy, boosting confidence and reducing feelings of helplessness. Setting and achieving fitness goals can translate to a greater sense of control and competence in other areas of life, reinforcing a mindset of resilience and fortitude.

Social Mechanisms

Participating in physical activities, especially in group settings, fosters social connections and support networks. These connections can provide emotional support, reduce feelings of isolation, and contribute to a sense of belonging, all of which are important for mental resilience.

Studies have consistently shown that regular physical activity can alleviate symptoms of depression and anxiety. A meta-analysis by Cooney et al. (2013) found that exercise is as effective as antidepressants for treating mild to moderate depression. Exercise also helps manage anxiety by reducing tension, improving sleep, and boosting self-esteem. Research indicates that physical activity reduces stress levels by lowering cortisol, the body's primary stress hormone. A study by Heaney et al. (2014) found that individuals who engage in regular physical exercise have lower baseline cortisol levels and exhibit a more adaptive response to acute stressors. Exercise has been linked to improved cognitive function, including better memory, attention, and executive function. A study by Colcombe and Kramer (2003) demonstrated that aerobic exercise enhances cognitive performance, particularly in older adults, by increasing brain volume in regions associated with memory and executive control.

Strategies for Building Physical Strength

1. **Set Clear Goals:** Setting clear, achievable goals is essential for maintaining motivation and tracking progress. Identify your strength training goals. These could be specific (e.g., lifting a certain weight, performing a certain number of repetitions) or general (e.g., improving overall fitness, increasing muscle mass). Write down your goals and break them into smaller, manageable steps.

2. **Develop a Balanced Routine:** A balanced routine includes exercises that target all major muscle groups and incorporates cardiovascular training, flexibility, and rest. Create a weekly workout plan that includes strength training exercises for different muscle groups (e.g., legs, back, arms, core), cardio sessions (e.g., running, cycling), and flexibility exercises (e.g., yoga, stretching). Ensure you include rest days to allow your muscles to recover.

3. **Focus on Proper Form:** Proper form is crucial to prevent injuries and maximize the effectiveness of your workouts. Before starting any new exercise, research the proper form or seek guidance from a fitness professional. Perform exercises slowly and with control, focusing on technique rather than speed or weight.

4. **Gradually Increase Intensity:** To build strength, you need to progressively increase the intensity of your workouts. Gradually increase the weight, resistance, or repetitions of your exercises. For example, if you are lifting weights, start with a manageable weight and gradually increase it as you become stronger. This principle of progressive overload ensures continuous improvement.

5. **Incorporate Recovery Strategies:** Recovery is an essential part of any strength training program. It helps prevent injuries and allows your muscles to repair and grow. Incorporate recovery techniques such as stretching, foam rolling, and adequate hydration. Ensure you get enough sleep and consider practices like massage or meditation to support overall recovery.

Remember, physical strength is not just about lifting weights; it is about lifting your life to new heights of wellness and vitality. Especially when you do not know where to start rebuilding your life. This is the most tangible way to stand back up.

9. Produce High-Quality Work

High-quality work not only brings a sense of personal satisfaction and achievement but also earns respect and trust from others. Producing high-quality work also aligns with the Stoic principles by creating a sense of purpose, resilience, and inner strength. By focusing on excellence in one's efforts, one demonstrates the virtues of diligence and integrity. This dedication to high-quality work is not merely about external success but about cultivating an inner discipline that strengthens character and fortitude. Through the process of striving for excellence, individuals learn to manage their impulses, control their responses to external events, and maintain a sense of calm and clarity, all of which are essential for enduring life's challenges with grace and resilience.

Moreover, Stoicism teaches that true fulfillment comes from within, through the pursuit of personal growth and virtue, rather than external rewards. By committing to producing high-quality work, one practices the Stoic principle of focusing on what is within one's control. This approach reduces anxiety and stress related to outcomes and external validation, as the emphasis is placed on the effort and intention behind the work rather than the results. High-quality work thus becomes a form of personal development, where each task is an opportunity to practice patience, perseverance, and excellence. This internal focus not only leads to better work but also builds a resilient mindset capable of withstanding setbacks and adversities, ultimately contributing to a more fortified and virtuous life.

It reflects dedication, resilience, and a commitment to excellence, even in the face of adversity. In a world where mediocrity is often the norm, producing high-quality work sets you apart and contributes to personal and professional growth. High-quality work enhances your professional reputation. It builds trust with colleagues, clients, and employers, leading to more opportunities and career advancement. Consistently delivering excellent work establishes you as a reliable and valuable contributor. Producing high-quality work brings a sense of personal satisfaction and pride.

When you produce high-quality work, you experience a sense of accomplishment that boosts self-esteem and self-efficacy. And as we mentioned earlier in this book, according to Bandura's theory of self-efficacy, believing in your ability to succeed in specific tasks can enhance your overall resilience and willingness to tackle challenges.

A study by Wrzesniewski et al. (1997) found that people who view their work as a calling—regardless of the job—experience higher job satisfaction and life satisfaction. This sense of calling is often linked to producing high-quality work. If excellence is one of your personal values, then this will give you a sense of purpose, contributing to overall life satisfaction and meaning. Engaging deeply with your work and striving for excellence can provide a profound sense of fulfillment and fortitude.

Principles of High-Quality Work

- **Attention to Detail:** Attention to detail ensures accuracy and completeness in your work. It involves thoroughness and care in every task, minimizing errors and enhancing the overall quality of your output.

- **Consistency:** Consistency in your work habits and output builds reliability. It means maintaining high standards across all tasks and projects, ensuring that every piece of work you produce meets the same level of excellence.

- **Continuous Improvement:** A commitment to continuous improvement drives you to refine your skills and processes continually. It involves seeking feedback, learning from mistakes, and staying updated with industry trends and best practices.

- **Integrity:** Integrity in your work means adhering to ethical standards and principles. It involves honesty, transparency, and accountability, ensuring that your work is trustworthy and credible.

Few things that you can utilize in order to produce high quality work:

1. **Leverage Your Intrinsic Motivation:** Intrinsic motivation refers to engaging in activities because they are inherently interesting and enjoyable, rather than for external rewards. This type of motivation is crucial for producing high-quality work because it fosters engagement, creativity, and persistence. A study by Deci and Ryan (2000) demonstrated that individuals who are intrinsically motivated perform better, are more innovative, and have higher job satisfaction. Identify aspects of your work that you find genuinely interesting and align them with your personal values and passions. Focus on the joy of learning and mastering new skills. If you're working on a challenging project, find elements within the project that excite you or align with your personal interests. This could be

the opportunity to learn a new technology or the chance to solve a complex problem.

2. **Embracing Deliberate Practice:** Deliberate practice involves focused, goal-oriented practice with the intent of improving performance. It requires breaking down tasks into smaller components, seeking feedback, and continuously refining your skills. Anders Ericsson's research on deliberate practice highlights that high achievers in any field engage in deliberate practice, which is structured, purposeful, and designed to improve performance. Break your work into specific skills or tasks. Set clear, measurable goals for improvement, and seek regular feedback. Focus on areas that challenge you and push you out of your comfort zone. If you're a writer, instead of just writing for the sake of writing, focus on specific aspects such as improving your narrative flow, enhancing character development, or refining your editing skills. Regularly review and critique your work to identify areas for improvement.

3. **Utilizing the Flow State:** Flow is a state of complete immersion and concentration in an activity, where time seems to fly by, and you perform at your best. Achieving flow can lead to high-quality work and greater satisfaction. Mihaly Csikszentmihalyi's research on flow states shows that people are most productive and creative when they are fully engaged in an activity that challenges their skills without overwhelming them. Create an environment that minimizes distractions and allows for deep focus. Choose tasks that are challenging but attainable, and set clear goals to guide your efforts. If you're working on a complex project, allocate uninterrupted time blocks during your peak productivity hours. Remove

distractions like phone notifications, and immerse yourself fully in the task at hand.

4. **Applying Design Thinking:** Design thinking is a human-centered approach to innovation that involves understanding the user, challenging assumptions, and redefining problems to identify alternative strategies and solutions. Research by Brown (2008) indicates that design thinking fosters creativity and innovation, leading to high-quality solutions that meet user needs more effectively. Approach your work with a design thinking mindset. Empathize with the end-user, define the problem clearly, brainstorm creative solutions, prototype, and test iteratively. If you're developing a new product or service, start by deeply understanding the needs and pain points of your target audience. Create prototypes and gather feedback to refine your solution continuously.

5. **Practicing Mindful Work:** Mindfulness involves being fully present and engaged in the current task, which can enhance focus, reduce stress, and improve the quality of work. Studies by Kabat-Zinn (2003) show that mindfulness practices can improve attention, cognitive performance, and emotional regulation. Integrate mindfulness practices into your daily work routine. Practice mindful breathing, take short mindfulness breaks, and fully engage with each task without multitasking. Before starting a task, take a few deep breaths to center yourself. During work, if your mind starts to wander, gently bring your focus back to the present moment. This practice can enhance your concentration and the quality of your work.

6. **Leveraging Interdisciplinary Learning:** Interdisciplinary learning involves drawing knowledge and skills from multiple disciplines to foster creativity and innovation. This approach can lead to more comprehensive and high-quality work. Research by Gawande (2014) suggests that interdisciplinary approaches can lead to breakthroughs and more holistic solutions by combining diverse perspectives. Explore and integrate concepts from different fields into your work. This can involve reading widely, attending interdisciplinary workshops, or collaborating with professionals from other domains. If you're a software developer, learn about psychology and design principles to create more user-friendly and effective software. This integration of knowledge can lead to higher quality and more innovative products.

10. Mix your Obsession with Patience

Obsession and patience might seem like polar opposites—one driven by intense focus and urgency, the other by calm perseverance and endurance. However, combining these two qualities can create a powerful synergy that fuels long-term success and resilience.

In sports, the concepts of choking and clutch performance illustrate the delicate balance between obsession and patience. Choking occurs when an athlete, often under intense pressure, fails to perform to their usual standard, despite their obsessive dedication to training and preparation. This is typically a result of anxiety and overthinking, which can paralyze performance. On the other hand, clutch performance is when an athlete excels under pressure, delivering their best performance when it matters most. This ability to perform in high-stakes situations reflects not only their obsession with perfecting their skills but also their patience and composure under pressure. Psychological research highlights that athletes who can maintain focus and stay calm, often through mindfulness and mental conditioning, are more likely to perform clutch plays rather than choke.

Mixing obsession with patience is crucial in transforming potential choke situations into clutch moments. An athlete's obsessive drive ensures they put in the necessary hours of practice and develop a deep passion for their sport. However, without the patience to remain composed and trust in their training during critical moments, this obsession can lead to anxiety and performance breakdowns. The key lies in blending intense preparation with the ability to stay present and manage stress effectively. It also aligns with the core principles of wisdom, courage, and temperance. True fortitude involves not only striving for excellence but also enduring challenges with equanimity.

Obsession without patience can lead to frustration and burnout, while patience without obsession may result in complacency. The balance of these traits reflects the ideal of living in harmony with nature and reason.

Marcus Aurelius, in his "Meditations," often reflected on the importance of perseverance combined with rationality. He believed that individuals should be unwavering in their pursuit of virtuous goals but also remain patient and resilient when faced with obstacles. This balance is essential for maintaining inner tranquility and achieving lasting success. By embodying this Stoic principle, we can ensure that our obsessive pursuits are guided by patience, allowing us to navigate setbacks and delays without losing sight of our ultimate objectives.

Seneca also emphasized the value of patience and fortitude in his letters. He argued that true strength lies in the ability to endure hardship with grace and maintain a steady course towards one's goals. This Stoic approach to resilience teaches us that patience is not a passive state but an active engagement with challenges, marked by a steadfast commitment to our principles and objectives. By integrating patience into our obsessive pursuits, we cultivate a deeper sense of purpose and resilience, enabling us to face life's trials with unwavering determination and calm.

Obsession, when directed positively, is a powerful force that can drive us to excel and achieve extraordinary results. It fuels our passion, keeps us motivated, and pushes us to pursue our goals relentlessly. Passion is a key component of this drive. When we are passionate about something, we naturally become more obsessed with it, dedicating significant time and effort to its pursuit. Research by Vallerand and colleagues distinguishes between harmonious passion, which leads to positive outcomes, and obsessive passion, which can lead to negative outcomes. Harmonious passion allows us to engage deeply and joyfully in our pursuits, leading to high-quality work and sustained effort. For instance, an artist who spends hours perfecting their craft, driven by a love for creating, embodies this harmonious passion.

Deep work, a concept popularized by Cal Newport, refers to focused, uninterrupted work on cognitively demanding tasks. Obsession with a goal often leads to engaging in deep work, where we immerse ourselves fully in our pursuits. Newport argues that deep work is essential for producing high-quality work and achieving significant results. This type of intense focus allows individuals to engage in complex problem-solving and develop expertise in their field. For example, a researcher obsessed with finding a cure for a disease may spend long hours in the lab, deeply focused on experiments and data analysis. This intense dedication can lead to groundbreaking discoveries and innovations.

The Necessity of Patience: Cultivating Endurance

While obsession drives us to pursue our goals with intensity, patience ensures that we can sustain our efforts over the long term. Patience allows us to navigate setbacks, delays, and challenges with resilience and grace. Patience is the ability to tolerate delays, obstacles, and discomfort without becoming frustrated or discouraged. It is a crucial component of emotional regulation and long-term success. A study by Sweeny and Falkenstein found that patience is associated with higher levels of well-being and life satisfaction, helping individuals manage stress and maintain a positive outlook during difficult times. For example, an entrepreneur building a business must exhibit patience as they navigate the uncertainties and setbacks of the startup world. Patience allows them to stay focused and persistent despite initial failures.

Delayed gratification, the ability to resist immediate rewards in favor of larger, long-term benefits, is closely linked to patience and is a key predictor of success. The famous Stanford marshmallow experiment by Mischel demonstrated that children who were able to delay gratification tended to have better life outcomes, including higher academic achievement and better health. For instance, a student preparing for a major exam must practice delayed gratification, choosing to study diligently over indulging in leisure activities. This patience and self-control lead to better academic performance and a deeper understanding of the material.

Mixing Obsession with Patience: The Synergy

When obsession is tempered with patience, you achieve a balanced approach that combines relentless pursuit with thoughtful endurance. This blend ensures that your efforts are intense and sustainable, allowing you to make consistent progress toward your goals without burning out or becoming disheartened by setbacks. Grit, a concept developed by psychologist Angela Duckworth, embodies this blend of obsession and patience. Grit is the combination of passion and perseverance for long-term goals. Duckworth's research shows that grit is a significant predictor of success in various domains, including education, military training, and professional achievement. Individuals with high levels of grit are more likely to achieve their long-term goals because they persist through challenges with both obsession and patience. For example, a marathon runner training for a race demonstrates grit by combining their obsession with running (passion) with the patience required to train consistently over months or years.

In the pursuit of fortitude, blending obsession with patience is not merely about balancing two seemingly opposing forces but about creating a synergistic relationship where each enhances the other. Let's look at some strategies which can help in creating the same.

1. **The Concept of Slow Mastery:** The concept of slow mastery involves immersing yourself deeply in the learning process, accepting that true expertise develops over time through deliberate and reflective practice. This approach contrasts sharply with the fast-paced, results-oriented mindset often driven by obsessive tendencies. Adopt an artist's mindset, where the focus is on perfecting each small component of your work. This might mean spending months or even years mastering a single aspect of your field before moving on to the next. Embrace the process of slow, deliberate practice without rushing for immediate results. A writer could focus on refining their ability to craft compelling dialogue for an extended period, experimenting with different techniques and styles, and reflecting deeply on the nuances of language and character interaction. This slow, patient approach ultimately leads to a higher quality of work and a deeper understanding of the craft.

2. **Integrate Stoic Practices into Daily Routine:** Stoic philosophy offers powerful tools for balancing the intense drive of obsession with the calm endurance of patience. Techniques like negative visualization and the dichotomy of

control help in managing emotions and maintaining focus on long-term goals. Practice negative visualization daily. Spend a few minutes imagining the potential obstacles and setbacks you might encounter in your pursuits. This prepares your mind for challenges and reduces the emotional impact of real setbacks, fostering patience. An entrepreneur might visualize the potential failure of a new product launch, considering all possible scenarios and outcomes. This exercise helps them remain calm and resilient if things don't go as planned, enabling them to continue their efforts with a balanced perspective.

3. **Engage in Micro-Progress Celebrations:** While long-term goals are essential, celebrating micro-progress can keep motivation high and reinforce the balance between obsession and patience. Recognizing small victories helps maintain enthusiasm and prevents burnout. Create a system of micro-rewards for incremental achievements. These rewards should be meaningful but not necessarily materialistic. They could be experiences, moments of reflection, or small personal indulgences. A software developer could reward themselves with a short break to play their favorite game after successfully debugging a complex piece of code. This practice not only celebrates progress but also integrates moments of relaxation and joy, sustaining their passion over the long term.

4. **Incorporate Cyclical Training Methods:** Cyclical training methods, often used in physical training, can be applied to mental and professional development. This involves alternating periods of intense focus with periods of rest and lower-intensity work, aligning with natural rhythms and preventing fatigue. Design your work schedule in cycles,

with periods of high intensity followed by deliberate low-intensity phases. This cyclical approach respects the natural ebb and flow of energy and concentration, promoting both obsession and patience. A researcher might have a month of intense data collection and analysis, followed by a month of reading, reflection, and conceptual development. This approach ensures that periods of intense work are balanced with time for recovery and deeper thinking.

5. **Utilize the Power of Reflective Journaling:** Reflective journaling allows you to process experiences, track progress, and maintain a dialogue with yourself. This practice can blend the intensity of obsession with the introspective patience needed for personal growth. Maintain a reflective journal where you document not just your achievements but also your thoughts, feelings, and lessons learned. Use this journal to identify patterns, celebrate progress, and plan incremental improvements. A musician might write daily reflections on their practice sessions, noting what worked, what didn't, and how they felt about their progress. Over time, this journal becomes a valuable tool for self-awareness and continuous improvement, merging their passion for music with the patience required for mastery.

11. Love yourself and your People from your Bare Soul

It is profoundly difficult to love and yet it is in our souls to do it like its breathing.

Patience, endurance, kindness, consideration, intellect and intuition, forgiveness and acceptance, courage and fearlessness—these virtues reside in all of us abundantly within our bare souls. However, our life adds layers of fear, impatience, insensitivity, ignorance, selfishness, cruelty, and resentment which gradually obscure these innate qualities. Beneath these layers, the true essence of love lies dormant.

Love, is one of the greatest acts of courage and **if you do it right**, it will make you powerful beyond your wildest imagination.

Nothing can drive your soul with more purpose than love.

What are you fighting against? May be your fate. But what are you fighting for? The answer to that has to be love. Loving from the bare soul means embracing ourselves and others without pretense or conditions. It is an unconditional acceptance and appreciation of our inherent worth and the intrinsic value of others. This form of love transcends superficial judgments and societal expectations, focusing instead on the essence of our being. Because when everything is lost, that is all that remains: bare soul. So you have to build your life driven by it, and around it. No expectations from society or any of your own superficial expectation will ever feed your soul and stay with you in the dark.

You need to love yourself and your people from the deepest core of your being where there is no place for judgement or expectations. Dr. Kristin Neff, one of the great researchers in the field of self-compassion, defines self-compassion as extending kindness and understanding to oneself in instances of pain or failure, rather than being self-critical. Self-compassion consists of three core components:

1. **Self-Kindness**: Treating oneself with care and understanding rather than harsh judgment. This involves recognizing that imperfection and suffering are part of the human experience and responding to oneself with warmth and support in difficult times.

2. **Common Humanity**: Acknowledging that suffering and personal inadequacy are part of the shared human experience. Recognizing that everyone makes mistakes and encounters difficulties can foster a sense of connectedness and reduce feelings of isolation.

3. **Mindfulness**: Holding one's painful thoughts and feelings in balanced awareness rather than ignoring them or exaggerating them. Mindfulness involves being open to the reality of the present moment and maintaining a non-judgmental stance towards one's experience.

Research has shown that self-compassion is associated with greater emotional resilience, lower levels of anxiety and depression, and a more positive outlook on life. It helps you to have a balanced perspective, reducing the likelihood of destructive self-criticism and enhancing overall well-being. Carl Rogers, a prominent humanistic psychologist, introduced the concept of unconditional positive regard as a fundamental component of psychological growth and self-acceptance.

Unconditional positive regard involves accepting and valuing a person without conditions or judgment.

This profound acceptance creates an environment where individuals feel safe to express their true selves, nurturing authenticity and personal development. When people feel accepted and valued without conditions, they are more likely to explore their potential and grow in positive directions.

Non-Judgmental Acceptance

At the heart of unconditional positive regard is non-judgmental acceptance. This entails accepting individuals exactly as they are, without evaluating or judging their worth. By offering acceptance without conditions, we create a supportive and nurturing environment that encourages personal growth. Our people are more likely to explore and develop their true selves when they do not fear judgment or rejection.

1. **Creating a Safe Space**: Non-judgmental acceptance helps create a safe space for individuals to express their thoughts, feelings, and experiences. When people feel safe from criticism or judgment, they are more likely to open up and be vulnerable, which is essential for personal growth and emotional healing.

2. **Promoting Self-Acceptance**: When individuals are accepted unconditionally by others, it promotes self-acceptance. This self-acceptance is crucial for mental health and well-being. People who accept themselves are more

resilient, have higher self-esteem, and are better able to cope with life's challenges.

3. **Encouraging Authenticity**: Non-judgmental acceptance encourages individuals to be authentic. When people feel they do not need to hide their true selves to be accepted, they are more likely to act in ways that are congruent with their values and beliefs. This authenticity leads to a more fulfilling and meaningful life.

Empathetic Understanding

Empathetic understanding is another vital component of unconditional positive regard. It involves striving to understand another's experience from their perspective. This empathetic approach helps individuals feel heard and validated, enhancing their self-worth and emotional well-being.

1. **Active Listening**: Empathetic understanding begins with active listening. This means fully concentrating on what the other person is saying, rather than planning your response. Active listening shows that you value the other person's experience and are genuinely interested in understanding them.

2. **Validation**: Empathetic understanding involves validating the other person's feelings and experiences. This does not necessarily mean agreeing with them, but rather acknowledging their perspective as valid and important. Validation helps individuals feel respected and valued, which is crucial for their self-worth.

3. **Emotional Resonance**: Empathetic understanding creates an emotional resonance between people. When we truly

understand and empathize with another person's experience, it creates a deep connection and fosters mutual trust. This emotional resonance is the foundation of strong and healthy relationships.

Genuineness

Genuineness, also known as congruence, is the third essential component of unconditional positive regard. Being genuine means being authentic and transparent in interactions, which encourages others to also be genuine and open. This mutual authenticity strengthens relationships and promotes deeper connections.

1. **Authentic Interactions**: Genuineness involves interacting with others in a way that is true to yourself. This means being honest about your thoughts and feelings, rather than hiding behind a façade. Authentic interactions build trust and respect, which are essential for healthy relationships.

2. **Consistency**: Genuineness also involves consistency between your words and actions. When your behavior aligns with your values and beliefs, it creates a sense of integrity and trustworthiness. Consistency helps others feel secure in the relationship, knowing that you are reliable and honest.

3. **Encouraging Openness**: When you are genuine, it encourages others to be open and authentic as well. This mutual openness creates a deeper level of connection and understanding, nurturing personal growth and strong, supportive relationships.

The impact of unconditional positive regard on personal development and relationships is profound. By embracing the principles of non-judgmental acceptance, empathetic understanding, and genuineness, we create an environment where unconditional positive regard thrives. This not only enhances individual well-being but also nurtures the development of deeper, more meaningful relationships.

1. **Nurturing Personal Growth**: Unconditional positive regard creates an environment that encourages personal growth and self-actualization. When individuals feel accepted and valued without conditions, they are more likely to explore their potential and strive towards their goals.

2. **Enhancing Mental Health**: Unconditional positive regard is associated with improved mental health outcomes. People who feel accepted and valued are less likely to experience anxiety and depression, and more likely to have higher self-esteem and resilience.

3. **Strengthening Relationships**: Unconditional positive regard strengthens relationships by fostering trust, respect, and mutual understanding. When people feel accepted and valued, they are more likely to form deep, meaningful connections with others.

To truly love from the bare soul, we must also understand our attachment styles and how they influence our interactions with others. Attachment theory, developed by John Bowlby and later expanded by Mary Ainsworth, provides a framework for understanding the emotional bonds we form in relationships. By recognizing our attachment styles and taking deliberate actions, we can learn to love more authentically and deeply.

Understanding Attachment Styles

Attachment styles are patterns of behavior and emotional responses that develop in early childhood based on our interactions with caregivers. These styles influence how we relate to others throughout our lives. There are four primary attachment styles:

1. **Secure Attachment**: Individuals with secure attachment feel comfortable with intimacy and independence. They trust others and have healthy, balanced relationships. Securely attached people are generally more resilient, have higher self-esteem, and are better at managing stress.

2. **Anxious Attachment**: Anxiously attached individuals often seek high levels of intimacy and approval from others, fearing abandonment and rejection. They may appear clingy or overly dependent in relationships, constantly seeking reassurance and validation.

3. **Avoidant Attachment**: Those with avoidant attachment tend to be emotionally distant and self-reliant. They often avoid close relationships and intimacy, fearing vulnerability and dependency. They may struggle with expressing emotions and prefer to keep others at arm's length.

4. **Disorganized Attachment**: Disorganized attachment is characterized by a mix of anxious and avoidant behaviors, often resulting from trauma or inconsistent caregiving. Individuals with this attachment style may exhibit unpredictable or contradictory behaviors in relationships, struggling with trust and emotional regulation.

Identifying Your Attachment Style

Understanding your attachment style is the first step towards loving from the bare soul. Reflect on your past and current relationships to identify patterns in your behavior and emotional responses. Consider the following questions:

- How do you respond to intimacy and closeness in relationships?
- Do you often seek reassurance from your partner or fear abandonment?
- Are you comfortable expressing your emotions and needs?
- Do you tend to avoid emotional closeness or prefer independence over intimacy?
- How do you handle conflicts and stress in relationships?

By honestly answering these questions, you can gain insights into your attachment style and how it affects your interactions with others.

Taking Action to Love from the Bare Soul

Once you have identified your attachment style, you can take deliberate actions to love more authentically and deeply. Here are some strategies for each attachment style:

1. **For Secure Attachment**:
    - **Maintain Balance**: Continue to nurture a healthy balance of intimacy and independence in your relationships.

- **Maintain Communication**: Keep communication open and honest, addressing any issues that arise with empathy and understanding.
- **Support Growth**: Encourage personal growth for yourself and your partner, fostering a relationship that evolves and strengthens over time.

2. **For Anxious Attachment**:
   - **Build Self-Confidence**: Focus on building your self-esteem and confidence outside of your relationships. Engage in activities that bring you joy and fulfillment.
   - **Practice Self-Soothing**: Learn techniques to manage anxiety and self-soothe during times of stress or insecurity. Mindfulness, meditation, and journaling can be helpful.
   - **Set Healthy Boundaries**: Establish and maintain healthy boundaries in your relationships. Communicate your needs clearly and respect your partner's space and independence.

3. **For Avoidant Attachment**:
   - **Embrace Vulnerability**: Challenge yourself to be more open and vulnerable in your relationships. Share your thoughts and feelings with your partner, even if it feels uncomfortable.
   - **Build Trust**: Work on building trust in your relationships by being reliable, honest, and consistent. Show your partner that you are committed and trustworthy.

- **Seek Support**: Consider seeking therapy or counseling to explore the roots of your avoidant behaviors and develop healthier ways of connecting with others.

4. **For Disorganized Attachment**:

    - **Seek Professional Help**: Given the complexity of disorganized attachment, seeking professional help from a therapist or counselor can be incredibly beneficial. Therapy can help you understand and process past traumas and develop healthier relationship patterns.

    - **Create Stability**: Focus on creating stability and consistency in your life. Establish routines and practices that provide a sense of security and predictability.

    - **Develop Emotional Regulation**: Learn and practice emotional regulation techniques to manage intense emotions and reactions. Mindfulness, deep breathing, and grounding exercises can be effective.

The love from your bare soul, rooted in authenticity and compassion, will allows you to see beyond imperfections and fears, nurturing connections that are genuine and enduring. As you peel back the layers of our defenses and vulnerabilities, you will discover a boundless capacity for empathy, understanding, and joy.

Let this chapter serve as a reminder that ***true strength lies not in shielding ourselves from the world, but in courageously opening ourselves up to it**, allowing love to flow freely from the very core of our being*. In this love, we find the essence of fortitude and the transformative power of loving wholly and unconditionally.

12. Cherish the Neutral Moments in Life

Every morning, the tea comes to a boil, the fragrant aroma fills the kitchen. As the tea simmers, I take a moment to appreciate the quietness of the early hour. The world outside is still waking up, and there is a sense of peace that permeates the air. I pour the hot tea into my favorite glass, and with the first sip, I close my eyes and let the warmth spread through my body. I am fully present, savoring the rich flavors and the comforting heat. The process is deliberate and unhurried, allowing me to focus solely on the task at hand. This moment is not about achieving something great or overcoming a challenge; it is about being fully here, appreciating the simplicity and the tranquility. In these few minutes, I find a profound sense of contentment.

The act of making and drinking chai is a reminder that life's beauty often lies in the smallest, most ordinary moments. It is a neutral moment, but it is one that anchors me, providing a sense of stability and peace amidst the ever-changing landscape of my life.

Having fought and lost countless battles in my life, trying to learn from them and actively pursuing the next ones, I could very easily sense that I am only focusing on the significant events of my life. These battles and victories, though crucial, are only a part of the narrative. Between these peaks and valleys lies a vast landscape of neutral moments—times that neither elevate us to ecstatic highs nor plunge us into despairing lows. Yet, these neutral moments are the fabric of our daily existence, and cherishing them can transform our understanding of life.

Psychological research highlights that our mental well-being is not solely built on extraordinary events but significantly on our everyday experiences. Martin Seligman, a pioneer in positive psychology, emphasizes that lasting happiness is often found in the mundane and the routine rather than in extraordinary achievements or dramatic events.

Marcus Aurelius, in his meditations, frequently reflected on the importance of accepting life as it is, finding contentment in the everyday flow of events. The Stoics believed that by appreciating the ordinary, we cultivate a stable and resilient mind, unshaken by the highs and lows of life. Jon Kabat-Zinn, a leading figure in mindfulness-based stress reduction, advocates for being present in each moment without judgment. This presence allows us to savor simple pleasures—a quiet morning, a walk in the park, or a meal with loved ones. These moments, though neutral, contribute immensely to our overall well-being.

Neutral moments provide a sense of stability and continuity in our lives. They are the quiet undercurrent that carries us through the highs and lows. By cherishing these moments, we build resilience, finding strength and contentment in the present rather than constantly seeking fulfillment in future achievements or past memories.

Some ideas on how to cherish the neutral moments can be:

1. **Mindful Awareness**

Mindfulness is the practice of being present and fully engaged with whatever we are doing at the moment. It involves paying attention to our thoughts, feelings, and surroundings without judgment. By cultivating mindful awareness, we can start to notice and appreciate neutral moments.

Try a simple mindfulness exercise. Sit quietly and focus on your breath. Notice the sensation of the air entering and leaving your body. Pay attention to the sounds around you, the feeling of the chair beneath you, and the rhythm of your breath. This practice helps ground you in the present and enhances your ability to appreciate neutral moments.

2. **Gratitude Journaling**

Keeping a gratitude journal can shift our focus from what is lacking to what is present and sufficient. By regularly noting down things we are grateful for, we begin to recognize and appreciate the neutral moments that bring stability and contentment to our lives.

Each day, write down three neutral moments you are grateful for. These could be as simple as a pleasant conversation, a meal you enjoyed, or a moment of quiet. Over time, this practice will help you see the value in everyday experiences.

3. **Engage in Simple Joy**

Make time for activities that bring you simple joy. These activities do not need to be extravagant or time-consuming; they can be small, daily rituals that ground you in the present.

Enjoying a cup of chai can be a cherished neutral moment. Take the time to prepare your chai with care. Notice the aroma of the spices, the sound of the water boiling, and the warmth of the cup in your hands. Savor each sip and be fully present in the experience. This simple pleasure can bring a sense of peace and contentment.

4. **Reflect on Daily Experiences**

At the end of each day, take a moment to reflect on the neutral moments you experienced. This reflection can enhance your appreciation for the mundane and help you recognize the steady foundation they provide.

Before bed, think about your day and identify three neutral moments that were pleasant or meaningful. Reflect on why these moments stood out and how they contributed to your overall sense of well-being.

5. **Connect with Nature**

Spending time in nature can help us appreciate the beauty and tranquility of neutral moments. Nature's steady rhythm and timeless beauty remind us to slow down and savor the present.

Go for a walk in a park or garden. Pay attention to the sights, sounds, and smells around you. Notice the rustling leaves, the chirping birds, and the fresh air. Allow yourself to be fully present in the experience and appreciate the simple beauty of nature.

6. **Slow Down**

In our fast-paced world, slowing down can help us notice and savor neutral moments. Taking the time to walk slowly, eat mindfully, and engage in conversations without rushing allows us to be fully present and appreciate the ordinary.

Choose one activity each day to do slowly and mindfully. This could be eating a meal, walking, or even brushing your teeth. Focus on the sensations and experiences involved, and allow yourself to fully engage with the moment.

The neutral moments, often perceived as mundane or unremarkable, hold the power to ground us and provide a sense of stability in our lives. These quiet spaces between the highs and lows, the steady rhythm that carries us through life's changes, can develop a balanced perspective that is not swayed by fleeting emotions or external circumstances. This mindful approach to life encourages us to find joy and peace in the ordinary, transforming routine activities into meaningful experiences that contribute to our emotional and mental health.

Now, as we draw this book to a close, if you feel like I was able to transform your perspective about your life, then our journey together has just started.

You can go to **www.fortitudeforever.com**

And stay connected with me personally through my podcast and other initiatives. I have decided (actually, I had no choice, but) to dedicate my life towards learning about fortitude and inspiring others to fight their fate for what they truly deserve.

If you simply want to connect on Instragram, these are my accounts:

@alg_suyash

@fortitudeforeverpodcast

I hope to see you on my website, my Instagram and my podcast which is available on all platforms including Youtube, Spotify,

Apple Podcast and many more with the name: Fortitude Forever podcast.

For now, I want to leave you with this quote:

"Look fate in the eyes and say, 'I don't deserve this. Even if everyone and everything I ever loved abandoned me, I will not join them in this contempt. I will never abandon myself.' This act of defiance is a victory in itself. If not anything, at least you deserve that victory, and you shall claim it."

www.ingramcontent.com/pod-product-compliance
Lightning Source LLC
LaVergne TN
LVHW041841070526
838199LV00045BA/1385